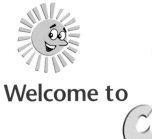

Welcome to

The leading authority on Places to take Children in the local area
researched & written by
Jill Taylor

This life saving guide supporting
Great Ormond Street Hospital Children's Charity
is not only packed with hundreds of ideas of places to go and things to do all year round, but also includes some first aid tips put together in association with the British Red Cross. You could save a life so find out how you can learn first aid.

Thoroughly researched and updated by local researcher Jill Taylor, who knows what children will enjoy, information is divided into chapters of subject interest. Check out Farms, Wildlife & Nature Parks, Sports & Leisure, History, Art & Science, Adventure & Fun, Trips, a fantastically useful chapter on Free Places for when you need to keep to a strict budget, and more on Places to Go further afield.

Whether you want to plan a special treat at a large adventure or theme park, try out a new sporting activity, step back in time to bygone eras, hire bikes or a boat or plan a hike and a picnic in the beautiful English countryside you will find all the information you need within the following pages, including price guide and opening information, where available.

Whatever the weather there is something to do summer or winter, rain or shine for an afternoon, a weekend or the long school holidays.

ALL YOU HAVE TO DO NOW IS GET UP AND GO OUT!

Enjoy some great days out with the children you care for.

With best wishes from
THE 'LET'S GO WITH THE CHILDREN' TEAM

Researched & written by JILL TAYLOR   **Edited by** LIN COOKSLEY
Advertising by JEANNETTE SANDISON   **Cover & Image design by** TED EVANS
Printed by Pims Print
Published by CUBE PUBLICATIONS
1 Cross Street, Aldershot GU11 1EY   **Telephone:** 01252 322771
www.cubepublications.co.uk   **Email:** enquiries@cubepublications.co.uk
5th Edition   ISBN   1 903594 46 4

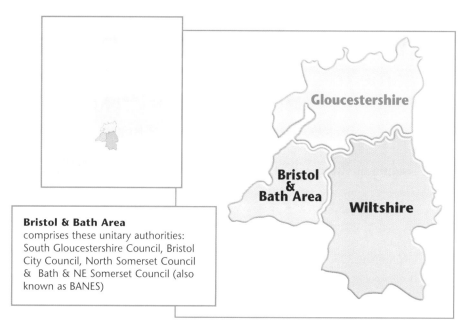

Bristol & Bath Area
comprises these unitary authorities:
South Gloucestershire Council, Bristol
City Council, North Somerset Council
& Bath & NE Somerset Council (also
known as BANES)

Colour Coding

Each county in this edition is colour coded as shown on the map above. Within each chapter the county areas and town names are colour coded in the same way so you always know where you are. Choose somewhere to go and use a good geographical map, such as an Ordnance Survey map, to help you find your way. Let your children help with the map reading. It will open up another world of adventure!

Great Ormond Street Hospital

Great Ormond Street Hospital for Children (GOSH) opened its doors on 14 February 1852. At the time it was the only centre for children's health in the country and had just 20 beds. Today the hospital is a world-renowned centre of excellence and treats over 90,000 sick children every year. Old buildings constantly need upgrading and a major redevelopment scheme was started in 2002. It will see one third of the existing site rebuilt, as well as the creation of some new facilities that will be dedicated to various aspects of modern care for children resulting in a 20% increased capacity.

Great Ormond Street Hospital Children's Charity (GOSHCC) aims to raise £20 million each year to fund the ongoing redevelopment as well as help buy state of the art medical equipment, fund research and provide support services, such as parent accommodation, for the young patients and their families.

We are proud to announce that a 6p contribution will be made for each 'Let's Go with the Children' guide sold this season. This year we are helping to fund a new area of parent accommodation in the hospital's new transitional care centre. These rooms will be used for parents whose children have come to GOSH for investigative procedures which will take more than 24 hours to complete and will allow parents to be closer to their children. This in turn makes for a less stressful visit to the hospital which can aid recovery.

You can get involved in other ways to help fund raise for GOSHCC. Check out www.gosh.org or call 0207 916 5678 for information.

Contents

Useful information

LOCAL COUNCILS

Local Councils look after a range of leisure facilities, many of which are featured in this guide, from play areas and skateparks to leisure centres and museums. Councils may be able to provide further information on special events and playschemes organised for children, particularly in the school holidays.

BRISTOL & BATH AREA: Bath & North East Somerset Council 01225 477000, Bristol City Council 0117 922 2000, North Somerset Council 01934 888888, South Gloucestershire Council 01454 868686.

GLOUCESTERSHIRE: Gloucestershire County Council 01452 425000, Cheltenham Borough Council 01242 262626, Cotswold District Council 01285 623000, Forest of Dean District Council 01594 810000, Gloucester City Council 01452 522232, Stroud District Council 01453 766321, Tewkesbury Borough Council 01684 295010.

WILTSHIRE: Wiltshire County Council 01225 713000, Kennet District Council 01380 724911, North Wiltshire District Council 01249 706111, Salisbury District Council 01722 336272, Swindon Borough Council 01793 463000, West Wiltshire District Council 01225 776655.

South Gloucestershire Council has launched a new website bringing together events and activities for the whole community, making it easier than ever before to find out what's going on in the area. The website **www.southglos.gov.uk/whatson** includes holiday activities for children at leisure centres, libraries, community centres and many more venues. Search by venue, age or type of activity to help you find exactly what you are looking for. South Gloucestershire's 14 libraries and 4 leisure centres have full programmes for children during holiday times, offering great value for money, so make sure you pay the site a visit to discover what's on at your nearest venue. **Check out inside back cover.**

TOURIST INFORMATION CENTRES

Tourist Information Centres can advise on local events and accommodation for visitors, they also stock colour leaflets about many of the attractions featured in this guide.

BRISTOL & BATH AREA: Bath: 0906 711 2000. Bristol: 0906 711 2191. Gordano: 0906 802 0806. Thornbury: 01454 281638. Weston-super-Mare: 01934 888800.

GLOUCESTERSHIRE: Bourton-on-the-Water: 01451 820211. Cheltenham: 01242 522878. Cirencester: 01285 654180. Coleford: 01594 812388. Gloucester: 01452 396572. Newent: 01531 822468. Stow on the Wold: (Cotswold) 01451 831082. Stroud: 01453 760960. Tetbury: 01666 503552. Tewkesbury: 01684 295027.

WILTSHIRE: Amesbury: 01980 622833. Avebury: 01672 539425. Bradford-on-Avon: 01225 865797. Chippenham: 01249 706333. Corsham: 01249 714660. Devizes: 01380 729408. Malmesbury: 01666 823748. Marlborough: 01672 513989. Melksham: 01225 707424. Mere: 01747 861211. Salisbury: 01722 334956. Swindon: 01793 530328. Trowbridge: 01225 777054. Warminster: 01985 218548. Westbury: 01373 827158.

Please mention this guide when visiting attractions.

Snapshots of places to go

National Birds of Prey Centre p51

South Cotswold Megamaze p11

HorseWorld Visitors Centre p47

Jolly Roger Adventure p12

Bristol Zoo Gardens p47

Can't find a babysitter?

SitterS
0800 38 900 38

For Evening Babysitters
www.sitters.co.uk

Evening Babysitters with Professional Childcare Experience

Now you can find mature, friendly and reliable evening babysitters, available at short notice. For your reassurance we interview each babysitter in person and check all references thoroughly.

All Sitters babysitters have professional childcare experience and most are local authority registered childminders or professionally qualified nursery nurses.

How does Sitters' service work

When you make a booking we arrange for a babysitter to attend at the appointed time. At the end of the evening you pay the babysitter for the hours they have worked. Babysitting rates start from £4.50 per hour and vary depending on your area. There are no additional charges for travelling costs and all bookings are for a minimum of 4 hours.

Each time you book a babysitter we charge a nominal £4 booking fee to your credit card. You can register with Sitters free! Membership of just £12.75 for 3 months will only be charged _after_ your first sitting. Call us today - less than £1 per week is a small price ensure your children are in experienced hands.

Experienced Childcarers Needed

Sitters welcomes applications from suitable babysitters. You will need to be over 21, have professional childcare experience, your own transport and immaculate references. For more information and to register your interest phone 0800 38 900 38 or visit www.sitters.co.uk.

For more information, phone us FREE today

0800 38 900 38
or visit us at www.sitters.co.uk
Please quote Ref: LET'S GO

REC
Recruitment &
Employment
Confederation

We're in YELLOW PAGES

INVESTOR

This is the chapter for soft play centres, mazes, laser arenas, family fun-pools and great adventure play facilities. There are also model villages and railway exhibitions that are perfect for less strenuous entertainment.

Some family pubs have play areas that are open all day. Log onto www.brewstersrestaurants.co.uk to search for Fun Factories, www.thespiritgroup.com for Wacky Warehouses and www.millhouseinns.co.uk for Pirate Pete Playdens.

Age and height restrictions generally apply at play centres and laser arenas. If centres are busy, playtime may be limited.

BRISTOL & BATH AREA

Play facilities at Leisure Centres. There are soft play areas at Bath, Bradley Stoke, Easton, Filton, Kingswood, Portishead's Parish Wharf, Thornbury and Yate Leisure Centres and at South Wansdyke Sports Centre in Midsomer Norton. See listing in `Sports & Leisure' chapter for contact details.

Banwell, Court Farm Country Park, Wolvershill Road, just off M5 at Weston-super-Mare, www.courtfarmcountrypark.co.uk 01934 822383. Runner-up in a national farm attractions competition in 2002 and 2003, Court Farm is a wonderful mix of animals, fun and adventure play. Help bottle-feed baby animals and take a tractor or `Big Cat' ride. Explore huge indoor play barns and the outdoor Adventure Land, tackle the eight-acre maize maze in summer or relax in the café. With so many undercover attractions, there's plenty to do whatever the weather. Open Summer, daily, 10am-5.30pm, Winter, closed Mons. Schools Birthdays **Open all year** Price B **Check out page 10.**

Bath, Bath Sports & Leisure Centre, North Parade Road, 01225 462565, has a leisure pool with giant waterslide and flume as well as the Zany Zone for soft play. Birthdays **Open all year** Price P.

Bath(near), Great Western Maze, Newton St Loe, off A4 Globe roundabout, www.greatwesternmaze.com 07775 870728. Puzzle your way out of the maize and enjoy the courtyard games. Open daily, mid Jul-mid Sept. Please telephone for times. Birthdays **Price B.**

Bristol, The Alphabet Zoo, Winterstoke Road, Bedminster, 0117 966 3366. Indoor adventure on a massive scale includes nets, rope bridges, ball pools and a slide. Open daily, 10am-7pm. Birthdays **Open all year** Price A.

Castaways Children's Playland, Waters Road, Kingswood, 0117 961 5115. A magical land to explore. Open Tues-Sat, times vary, & Suns for parties only. Birthdays **Open all year** Price A.

Harry's Quasar Centre, All Saints Street, 0117 927 7671. Space-age adventure with laser guns. Pre-booking advised. Open daily, 10am-9pm. Birthdays **Open all year** Price P.

Laser Quest Bristol, The Old Fire Station, Silver Street, Broadmead, www.laserquest.info 0117 949 6688. Outwit the opposition in a game of laser tag. Check availability before visiting. Open daily, times vary. Birthdays **Open all year** Price P.

Mayhem, Riverside Leisure, Station Road, Little Stoke, 01454 888666, has a playframe complete with rope swing and bridges. Open daily, 10am-5.45pm. Birthdays **Open all year** Price A.

Megabowl Bristol, Brunel Way, Ashton Gate, www.megabowl.co.uk 0871 550 1010. Choose between adventure golf, bowling, pool, amusements and Planet Kids, a soft play area. Open daily, times vary. Birthdays **Open all year** Price P.

Bristol(near), Noah's Ark Zoo Farm, Failand Road, Wraxall, between Bristol and Clevedon on the B3128, www.noahsarkzoofarm.co.uk 01275 852606, has superb adventure play areas and a hedge maze. **Check out 'Farms' chapter and page 50.**

Keynsham, Avon Valley Country Park, www.avonvalleycountrypark.co.uk 0117 986 4929, covers 32 acres and has animals, outdoor and undercover play areas, an assault course, mini quad bikes, boating and mini steam train rides. Open end Mar-Oct, Tues-Sun, Bank Hol Mons, & daily in school hols, 10am-6pm; Winter (indoor play area only), Sat-Sun & school hols, 10am-5pm. Birthdays **Open all year Price B.**

Midsomer Norton, Panda-monium, Pows Orchard, 01761 419091, is a soft play centre. Telephone for opening times. Birthdays **Open all year Price A.**

Weston-super-Mare, Grand Pier, 01934 620238. A traditional pier with covered amusement park. Entertainment for all ages includes a free-fall ride, ghost train, adventure playground, soft play area, dodgems and bowling. Open mid Feb-end Oct, 10am-6pm (closes 10pm in high season), days vary. **Price P.**

The Great Weston Train Experience, Clifton Road, www.modelmasters.co.uk 01934 629717. A European model railway exhibition at the back of a shop. Amazing detail in scenes that range from a modern city station to snow-covered mountains. Re-opening mid Jul 2005, telephone for details.

Weston Park Raceway, www.westonparkraceway.co.uk - relocating early 2005 – has slot-car racing tracks. Check website for details. Birthdays **Open all year Price P.**

GLOUCESTERSHIRE

Play facilities at Leisure Centres. Younger children will enjoy the permanent soft play areas at Cheltenham's Leisure@cheltenham and Stroud's Stratford Park Leisure Centre – see listing in 'Sports & Leisure' chapter for contact details.

Berkeley(near), **Cattle Country Adventure Park,** www.cattlecountry.co.uk 01453 810510. Look out for the drop slide! This is a family day out with huge indoor and outdoor play areas, a herd of American bison, pets corner, a willow maze and farm trail. Telephone for opening times. Schools Birthdays **Open all year Price C.**

Bourton-on-the-Water, **Bourton Model Railway Exhibition,** High Street, www.bourtonmodelrailway.co.uk 01451 820686. The railways run through incredibly detailed background scenery. Press the buttons and watch them come to life. Open Apr-Sept, daily, 11am-5pm, Oct-Mar, Sat-Sun. Limited opening in Jan. **Open all year Price A.**

Dragonfly Maze, Rissington Road, 01451 822251. Solve all the clues and your reward will be a glimpse of the Golden Dragonfly in the centre. Open daily from 10am, closing times vary. Check Jan-Feb opening. **Open all year Price A.**

Fundays, Bourton Industrial Park, www.fundaysplaybarn.com 01451 822999. Ball ponds, nets, slides, tubes and soft play give masses of scope for indoor adventure. Laser tag available for parties only. Open daily, 10am-6pm. Birthdays **Open all year Price B.**

Model Village, The Old New Inn, www.theoldnewinn.co.uk 01451 820467, is a 1/9 scale replica of Bourton-on-the-Water built in Cotswold stone, complete with the model of the model village and singing from the church. Go through a turnstile (extra £1 per person) to enter **Miniature World,** full of delightful scenes. Open daily, Summer, 9am-5.45pm, Winter, 10am-3.45pm. **Open all year Price A.**

Cheltenham, **Ballyhoo,** Chosen View Road, 01242 252205. Flop in the ball pit after sliding, crawling and swinging around this large adventure play centre. Laser tag birthday parties available. Open daily, 10am-6pm. Birthdays **Open all year Price B.**

Chipping Campden(near), **Hidcote Manor Farm Maize Maze,** Hidcote Bartrim, www.hidcotemaze.co.uk 01386 430178. Pack a picnic and spend an entire day in the fresh air. Open late Jul-mid Sept, telephone for details.

Cirencester, **MagicLand,** Meadow Road, www.magicland.co.uk 01285 885570, is a huge soft play centre with a cannon arena, thrilling slides and a small football pitch to keep everyone happy. Open daily, 10am-6.30pm. Birthdays **Open all year Price A.**

Coleford, **Little Follies,** Mile End Road, www.littlefollies.co.uk 01594 833229. Race around a three-level indoor playground with a trampoline or challenge your friends to ten-pin bowling and air hockey. Open daily, 10am-6pm. Birthdays **Open all year Price P.**

Coleford(near), **Puzzle Wood,** on B4228 Chepstow Road, 01594 833187. The deep ravines, wooden bridges and moss-covered rocks of this maze create a magical landscape. Not suitable for pushchairs. Indoor Wood Puzzle and farm animals. Open Easter-Oct, Tues-Sun & Bank Hol Mons, 11am-5.30pm (4pm Oct). Schools **Price B.**

Gloucester, **Dark Light Laser Tag,** at JDR Karting, 5 Madleaze Industrial Estate, Bristol Road, www.lasertaggloucester.com 01452 311211. Stalk your opponents with a laser gun. Karting also available and pre-booking advisable. Open daily, times vary. Birthdays **Open all year Price P.**
House of the Tailor of Gloucester, 9 College Court, 01452 422856, is now a shop with a definitive range of Beatrix Potter merchandise and a small display of pictures and models. Open Mon-Sat, 10am-5pm (4pm Nov-Mar). Closed Bank Hols. **Open all year Price A.**
Jesters Play Centre, Matson Lane, 01452 383077, has a playframe and bouncy castle. Open daily, 10am-6pm. Birthdays **Open all year Price A.**
Kidzone, Great Western Road, 01452 422373. Family entertainment with pool and air hockey as well as a multilevel playframe and bouncy castle. Open daily, 9.30am-6.30pm. Birthdays **Open all year Price P.**
LaughterLand, Quedgeley Enterprise Centre, Naas Lane, Quedgeley, 01452 729722. Cargo nets, ball pools, ropes and slides for action and excitement. Open daily, 10am-5pm. Birthdays **Open all year Price A.**
PlayZone, Riverside Sports & Leisure Club, St Oswald's Road, www.riversidesports.co.uk 01452 413214. Indoor fun on a two-level playframe. Telephone for opening times. Birthdays **Open all year Price A.**

Longhope, **Mohair Countryside and Dick Whittington Centre,** Little London, 8 miles W of Gloucester, off A40, www.royal-forest-of-dean.com/mohair 01452 831137. Meet Grunty the Pig and his farm friends plus Bambi and the deer. Explore 100 acres of countryside and then visit the play zones. Outside are a giant sandpit, pedal course, adventure play zone and adjacent picnic area. The indoor area covers approximately 800 square metres and includes play equipment with slides, trampolines and ball pools, the Toy Corner, Farm and Rural Information Corner, gift shop and restaurant. Most suitable for toddlers to ten-year-olds. Open daily in school hols, 10am-5pm. Closed Mon-Tues in term time. Schools Birthdays **Open all year Price B Check out page 10.**

Lydney(near), **Forest of Dean Model Village & Gardens,** Lydney Park Estate, www.forest-model-village.co.uk 01594 845244. A charming representation of Forest life with sheep on a zebra crossing and many humorous touches. Open Easter-end Oct, check website for times. Schools Birthdays **Price B.**

Stroud, **Go Bananas Soft Play,** Ebley Wharf, 01453 769120. The wavy astra slide is bound to be a favourite here. Open Mon-Fri, 9.30am-6pm, Sat-Sun, 10am-6pm. Birthdays **Open all year Price A.**

Symonds Yat West, **Amazing Hedge Puzzle,** Jubilee Park, www.mazes.co.uk 01600 890360, is just over the border into Herefordshire. Find the centre of the maze, solve lots of puzzles in the museum or play hide and seek. On the same site is the recently opened Butterfly Zoo. Open daily, 11am-5pm or dusk if earlier. Schools Birthdays **Open all year Price B.**
Symonds Yat West Leisure Park, Jubilee Park, www.symondsyatleisure.co.uk 01600 890350, has a large outdoor play area and small fairground (open spring-autumn). There is a new indoor soft play centre with bouncy castles, shark slide, Noah's Ark, trampolines and more. Open daily, 10am-6pm. Schools Birthdays **Open all year Price P.**

Tewkesbury(near), **Playzone,** Croft Farm Leisure and Water Park, Bredons Hardwick, www.playzone-tewkesbury.co.uk 01684 773873. This indoor activity centre has a playstructure and soft play area plus air hockey and football tables. Telephone for further details. Birthdays **Open all year.**

Westbury-on-Severn(near), **Elton Farm Maize Mazes,** Elton, www.eltonmaizemaze.co.uk 01452 760795, where one of the mazes is a water pistol maze! Leave time for the courtyard activities. Open mid Jul-mid Sept, 11am-6pm. Telephone to confirm. Birthdays **Price A/B.**

Wotton-under-Edge(near), **South Cotswold Megamaze,** Kingswood, www.megamaze.co.uk 01453 843120. Explore the amazing new maze for 2005! Find your way around more than two miles of trail carved through five acres of growing maize. Use the bridges to get a 3D effect and a bird's-eye view of the maze. Assistance is available if required. There is a picnic area in the courtyard with pedal karts for all ages, a giant haystack, mega sandpit, large trampoline and more. Light refreshments are available. Open daily, mid Jul-Sept, please see website or telephone for times. Available for private evening/group hire. Free admission for under 3s. **Price B Check out page 10.**

WILTSHIRE

Play facilities at Leisure Centres. Marlborough Leisure Centre and Tisbury & District Sports Centre have permanent soft play areas. The listing in the 'Sports & Leisure' chapter has contact details.

Ansty, **Ansty PYO and Farm Shop,** 01747 829072, has a maize maze in summer, PYO fruit in season, a tearoom and the Pumpkin Olympics during October half term. Birthdays.

Calne, **Jumping Jacks Indoor Play Centre,** Carnegie Road, Portemarsh Industrial Estate, 01249 822644. Bounce on the castle, explore the playframe or try soft football and basketball. Open Mon-Sat, 9.30am-6pm, Sun, 10.30am-6pm. Birthdays **Open all year Price A.**

Calne(near), **Bowood House, Gardens and Adventure Playground,** www.bowood.org 01249 812102. Combine historic learning and spectacular surroundings with the thrill of adventure for children aged two to twelve. The extensive 'Capability Brown' park includes a 40-acre lake, waterfall and cave, and provides ample space for games and picnics. The stately home itself houses fine displays of costume, family heirlooms and works of art. The superb Adventure Playground boasts a life-size pirate ship, high-level rope-walks, giant slides and the famous Space Dive. There is an indoor Soft Play Palace for younger children and birthday party packages are available. Open daily, 19th Mar-1st Nov, 11am-6pm or dusk if earlier. Schools Birthdays **Price B/C Check out 'History' chapter and page 10.**

Chippenham, **The Olympiad Leisure Centre,** Monkton Park, 01249 444144. Have fun in the pool with two waterchutes, rapids and water cannon. **Open all year Price A.**

Devizes, **Coral Cove,** Hopton Industrial Estate, 01380 739944. Whoosh down the slide and wade through the ball pool on your way around this multi-tier playstructure. Open Mon-Sat, 9.30am-6pm (7pm Fri-Sat), Sun, 10am-5pm. Birthdays **Open all year Price A.**

Melksham, **Boomerang,** Merlin Way, Bowerhill, 01225 702000, provides lots of indoor entertainment with a giant adventure frame, soft play area, laser games and games zone. Laser games must be pre-booked. Open daily from 9am, closing times vary. Birthdays **Open all year Price P.**

Salisbury, **Outburst** (includes Clown About, Strikers and Laser A), Unit 5, Milford Trading Estate, Blakey Road, www.outburstsalisbury.com 01722 413121. With an exciting two-level playstructure, laser tag and bowling, there is something for all the family. Open daily, times vary. Birthdays **Open all year Price P.**

Swindon, Jolly Roger Adventure, Greenbridge Road, www.jollyrogerplay.com 01793 522044. One of the biggest indoor play centres in the South with bouncy castles, an amazing soft adventure play area and a live Amazon parrot called Charlie! Go for a dip in one of the ball pools, squeeze between rollers or mess about in the biff and bash bags, webbed tunnels and `Little Tikes' area. A popular recent addition is a three-lane astra slide that is seriously fast and long. For the very brave (and this can include mum and dad), there's a fearsome drop slide of over nine metres! While the children are using up all that energy, parents can sit back, relax and enjoy a cup of tea or coffee and a snack. The whole family can stay for dinner and there is a range of amusements and games for children of all ages. Birthday parties last for two hours and include 45 minutes in a private party room. Open Mon-Fri, 9am-6.30pm, Sat-Sun, 9.30am-6pm. Birthdays **Open all year Price A Check out inside front cover.**

Laser Quest Swindon, Fleetway House, Queen Street, www.lqswindon.co.uk 01793 567950. Battle it out with laser guns. Telephone to pre-book. Open daily, times vary. Birthdays **Open all year Price P.**

The Oasis Pool, Oasis Leisure Centre, North Star Avenue, 01793 445401. Are you brave enough for the Domebuster flumes? If not, there are gentler slides, a wave machine, water cannon and shallows for paddling. Birthdays **Open all year Price B.**

Space Adventure, Isis Trading Estate, Shrivenham Road, www.spaceadventure.co.uk 01793 422033. Soft and adventure play, human tabletop football, batak, gamecubes, sumo wrestling and laser tag are all under one roof. Some activities are for parties only. Open daily, times vary. Birthdays **Open all year Price P.**

Swindon(near), Bonkers, Studley Grange, Wroughton, www.studleygrange.co.uk 01793 855566, is part of the Craft Village. A fully interactive indoor play area for all ages with ball pool, toddler area, aerial glide, roller racers, ball cannons and more. Open Mon-Sat, 10am-5pm, Sun, 10.30am-4.30pm. Birthdays **Open all year Price P Check out 'Pottery Painting & Craft Activities' and page 20.**

The Really-Really Wild Club, The Swallow Hotel and Leisure Club, South Marston, 01793 833700, is a multi-tier, indoor soft play area. Outside is a small rustic adventure playground. Open daily, telephone for times. Birthdays **Open all year Price A.**

Warminster, Longleat, www.longleat.co.uk 01985 844400. The Longleat Hedge Maze is just one of many attractions. **Check out 'Farms' chapter and page 50.**

Tropical Park, Woodcock Industrial Estate, www.tropicalpark.co.uk 01985 847500. Join in the fun at an indoor activity centre for children up to 12 years. Scramble up cargo nets, play Tarzan on the rope swings, bounce on the castle, catch the aerial glide, wallow in ball ponds and shoot down the three-lane, wavy slide. The very young (0-4 years) can play undisturbed in a separate room with soft play, ball pond, gentle slide, wall puzzles and games. This spotlessly clean centre is no less a treat for parents with comfortable seating and tables, a cafeteria and strategically placed CCTV cameras around the multilevel playframe. A birthday party at Tropical Park means 90 minutes of fun for children and hassle-free entertaining for parents; food is provided with a private party room available. Friday nights are disco nights with two sessions for different age groups: 6-7.30pm for 5 to 12 year olds and 7.30-9.30pm for 12 to 16 year olds. An after-school club is planned for 2005. Open daily, 10am-5.30pm. Birthdays **Open all year Price A Check out outside back cover.**

Westbury, Jungle Jacks, Headquarters Road, West Wilts Trading Estate, 01373 824824. Use up surplus energy on the playstructure and then relax in the ball pools. Open daily, 10am-5.30pm. Birthdays **Open all year Price A.**

Westbury(near), Brokerswood Country Park, www.brokerswood.co.uk 01373 822238, is 80 acres of woodland with trails, two adventure playgrounds, a play trail, narrow-gauge railway (check operating times), undercover play area for younger children and heritage centre. Open daily, 10am-5pm. Schools Birthdays **Open all year Price A.**

Sports & Leisure

This chapter is packed with ideas for free time and birthday parties. Check out the activities at your local sports centre or try something totally different. Have a go at ice-skating or snowboarding, abseiling or kayaking. Get creative with pottery painting and crafts, watch first-class sport or visit the theatre.

Abbreviations: A: Archery, Ab: Abseiling, AC: Assault Course, Ba: Banana Boats, BB: Bridge Building, C: Canoeing, Cl: Climbing, Cm: Camping, Cv: Caving, GW: Gorge Walking, HW: Hill Walking, K: Kayaking, MB: Mountain Biking, MBd: Mountain Boarding, O: Orienteering, PS: Problem Solving, R: Riding, Ri: Ringoes, RsC: Ropes Course, Rt: Rafting Activities, S: Sailing, SB: Skate Boarding, Sn: Snorkelling, SnS: Snow Sports, TB: Team Building, W: Windsurfing, Wb: Wakeboarding, WS: Water Skiing, WSp: Water Sports.

ADVENTURE ACTIVITIES

See also 'Climbing' and 'Water Sports' listings.
BRISTOL & BATH AREA: Banwell: **Mendip Outdoor Pursuits** 01934 820518/823666 A Ab AC Cl Cv O PS WSp. Bristol: **The Adventurous Activity Company** Hotwell Rd 0117 925 3196 Ab Cl Cm HW MB O TB WSp, **Bristol Activities Centre** Cumberland Basin 0117 926 5850 (groups only) Ab Cl Cv HW MB O TB WSp, **Young Bristol Outdoor Activity Centre** Pooles Wharf 0117 953 7921 (groups only) Ab Cl Cv GW MB TB WSp. Churchill: **High Action Ltd** Lyncombe Dri 01934 852335 A Ab Cl MB MBd O R SB SnS.
GLOUCESTERSHIRE: Christchurch: **Forest Adventure Ltd** 01594 834661 (groups only) A Ab Cl Cv MB O PS WSp, **Motiva Ropes Course** 01594 861762 RsC. Cirencester(Cotswold Water Park): **Head 4 Heights** 01285 770007 RsC, **Waterland Outdoor Pursuits** 01285 861202 (groups only) A BB O WSp. Coleford: **Wyedean Canoe & Adventure Centre** 01594 833238 A Ab Cl Cv O PS RsC WSp. Lydney(near): **Wye Valley Quad Bikes Ltd** Tidenham 01291 689940 A.

ADVENTURE HOLIDAYS

PGL Activity Holidays, www.pgl.co.uk 08700 507 507, has 11 UK residential centres offering activity holidays for 7-10, 10-13 or 13-16 year olds covering football, drama, kayaking, 'Adrenaline Adventure', 'Learner Driver' and much more. There are also 'Family Active' holidays for all the family and centres in France. Winter snow sports are available in Austria. Telephone for free brochure. **Check out page 14.**

BOWLING (TEN-PIN)

BRISTOL & BATH AREA: Bristol: **Bowlplex** Aspects Leisure Pk Longwell Gr 0117 961 0000, **Hollywood Bowl** Avonmeads Retail Pk 0117 977 1777, **Megabowl Bristol** Brunel Way Ashton Gate 0871 550 1010. Weston-super-Mare: **AMF Weston** Dolphin Sq 0845 658 1288.
GLOUCESTERSHIRE: Cheltenham: **Cotswold Bowl** 2 Wymans La Kingsditch 01242 226766. Coleford: **Little Follies** Mile End Rd 01594 833229. Gloucester: **Minnesota Fats Sports Bar** The Peel Centre 01452 414962, **Tenpin Gloucester** Centre Severn Barnwood 0871 550 1010.
WILTSHIRE: Melksham: **Christie Miller Sports Centre** 32 Lancaster Rd Bowerhill 01225 702826. Salisbury: **Strikers** (at Outburst) Unit 5 Milford Trading Est Blakey Rd 01722 413121. Swindon: **Megabowl Swindon** Whitehill Way 0871 550 1010.

14

See 'Theatres & Arts Centres' also, as schedules often include films. Contact details for Odeon cinemas are given in the box below.
BRISTOL & BATH AREA: Bath: **Little Theatre** St Michael's Pl 01225 466822, **Odeon** Kingsmead Leisure Complex James St West. Bristol: **Cineworld** Hengrove Leisure Pk 0871 220 8000, **Cube** Dove St South 0117 907 4190, **Imax® Theatre-At-Bristol** Anchor Rd 0845 345 1235, **Odeon** Union St Broadmead, **Orpheus** Northumbria Dri Henleaze 0845 166 2381, **Showcase** Avonmeads Leisure Pk 0117 972 3800, **Vue** Aspects Leisure Pk Longwell Gr 0871 2240 240, **Vue** Cribbs Causeway 0871 2240 240, **Watershed Media Centre** 1 Canons Rd 0117 927 5100. Clevedon: **Curzon** Old Church Rd 01275 871000. Weston-super-Mare: **Odeon** The Centre.
GLOUCESTERSHIRE: Cheltenham: **Odeon** Winchcombe St. Cinderford: **The Palace** Belle Vue Rd 01594 822555. Coleford: **Studio** High St 01594 833331. Gloucester: **UGC** The Peel Centre Bristol Rd 0871 200 2000.
WILTSHIRE: Chippenham: **Astoria** Marshfield Rd 01249 652498. Devizes: **Palace** The Market Pl 01380 722971. Salisbury: **Odeon** New Canal. Swindon: **Cineworld** Greenbridge Retail Pk 0871 220 8000, **UGC** Shaw Ridge Leisure Pk Whitehill Way 0871 200 2000.

ODEON CINEMAS Hotline: 0871 22 44 007 www.odeon.co.uk

Also see 'Adventure Activities'.
BRISTOL & BATH AREA: Bristol: **Bristol Climbing Centre** Mina Rd 0117 941 3489.
GLOUCESTERSHIRE: Gloucester: **Warehouse Climbing Centre** Parliament St 01452 302351.
WILTSHIRE: Swindon: **Link Centre** Whitehill Way Westlea 01793 445566. Tidworth: **Tidworth Leisure Centre** Nadder Rd 01980 847140.

Little Mischiefs, 10 Causeway Head Road, Dore, near Sheffield 0114 262 1500/262 1020, offers a wide range of quality personalised gifts for babies, toddlers and parents. Also Lucy Locket fancy dress, Collins & Hall special occasion wear and limited edition handbags. Shop on-line at www.littlemischiefs.co.uk **Check out page 14.**

Bristol, **John Nike Leisuresport,** Bristol Ice Rink, Frogmore Street, www.jnll.co.uk 0117 929 2148, welcomes skaters of all types, from the absolute beginner to the dazzlingly proficient. Dust off your skates or hire a pair and get out onto the ice! There are public, family and disco sessions so pick the one that best suits your needs. Private lessons are available to get novices off to a flying start (advance booking essential), six-week Learn to Skate courses run regularly during term time and there is a Junior Ice Hockey Programme. The birthday party package (for a minimum of eight children) includes skate hire, half an hour of professional tuition, more time on the ice and then food in the cafeteria. Ice karting can be arranged for adults. Open daily, timetable varies. Birthdays **Open all year Check out page 16.**

WILTSHIRE: Swindon: **Link Centre** Whitehill Way Westlea 01793 445566.

KARTING

BRISTOL & BATH AREA: Bristol: **The Raceway** Avonmouth Way Avonmouth 0800 376 6111, **West Country Karting Ltd** Bradley Stoke 01454 202666.
GLOUCESTERSHIRE: Gloucester: **JDR Indoor Karting** 5 Madleaze Ind Est Bristol Rd 01452 311211.
WILTSHIRE: Castle Combe: **Skid Pan & Kart Track** 01249 783010. Salisbury(near): **Avago Karting** West Dean 01794 884693, **Wessex Raceway** Coombe Bissett 01725 519599. Swindon(near): **Swindon Karting** Area One Hackpen La Wroughton Airfield 01793 814340.

MUSIC & MOVEMENT

Jo Jingles, www.jojingles.co.uk 01494 719360, is a marvellous music and singing experience with an educational slant for children aged 6 months to 5 years. Exciting and stimulating classes run at venues all over the country. For details on classes in your area or for information on the franchise opportunity please call 01494 719360, email: headoffice@jojingles.co.uk or visit the website. Birthdays **Check out page 14.**

Monkey Music, www.monkeymusic.co.uk 01582 766464, runs music classes for babies and children aged between 6 months and 4 years at venues all over the UK. Please telephone for details of local classes. Birthdays **Check out page 16.**

Rhythm Time, www.rhythmtime.net 0121 711 4224, runs quality music classes for babies, toddlers and older children. Interesting new ideas and songs to help development and musical skills. Courses written by a music teacher. Classes opening all over the UK. For details or information about the exciting franchise opportunity please call or email kathy@rtfg.co.uk **Check out page 16.**

PAINTBALLING

Paintballing is suitable for older children only. It is popular with some teenagers and adults but it is important that you check out the organisation offering the activity for your children and be satisfied that proper safety regulations are observed. Most of the sites below are members of the United Kingdom Paintball Sports Federation (www.ukpsf.com), but the sport does not appear to be regulated. In all cases, parents should check suitability before booking.
BRISTOL & BATH AREA: Bristol(near): **Hamburger Hill** Bristol Outdoor Pursuits Centre Hunstrete 0800 980 3980, **Max Events Ltd** 07789 988881, **Paintball Adventures** near Lulsgate Airport 0117 935 3300. Portishead: **Skirmish Paintball Games** 01934 416507.
GLOUCESTERSHIRE: Cirencester: **Pro Ball Ltd** Cotswold Water Pk 01367 252433. Coleford: **Forest Combat** English Bicknor 01594 861757. Gloucester: **Paintball Raiders** Brookethorpe 01452 306117. Moreton-in-Marsh: **Cotswold Paintballing** 07836 657397. Winchcombe: **Winchcombe Paintball** 01242 604231.
WILTSHIRE: Swindon/Warminster: **Experience Paintball** 01380 728982.

Sprains and Strains
Signs and Symptoms:
- Pain
- Swelling
1. Make the child comfortable and raise the injured part.
2. To minimise swelling wrap a cold compress (icepack/frozen vegetables) in a cloth or towel. Hold against the injury for up to 30 minutes.
Seek medical advice if necessary.

Cheltenham, **Floating World,** 01242 863297, offers a wonderful selection of balloons for children's parties and will even decorate the venue for you. These are very special balloons designed to bring a touch of magic to any youngster's celebration. Why not present each guest with one to take home at the end? Especially popular are the character balloons. Party in the company of firm favourites like Winnie the Pooh, Thomas the Tank Engine, Nemo and Clifford! Balloons can be personalised for themed parties and special occasions. Whether your event is for small children, teenagers or adults, please telephone to discuss requirements. Discounts available for quantities or good causes. **Check out page 14.**

BRISTOL & BATH AREA: Bath: **Crock a doodle do** 78 Walcot St 01225 442700. Bristol: **Glaze 'n' Shine** 252 Soundwell Rd Kingswood 0117 330 1382, **Make Your Mark** 97 Whiteladies Rd Clifton 0117 974 4257. Chipping Sodbury: **Inspiration** 4 Beaufort Mews Horse St 01454 313011.

GLOUCESTERSHIRE: Cheltenham: **Paint It Yourself Pottery Co** Winchcombe St 01242 575700, **Purple Glaze** 10 Great Norwood St 01242 526863. Coleford: **Rainbow Pottery** St John's St 01594 811118, **Reckless Designs** 17 Gloucester Rd 01594 810504. Lydney: **Taurus Crafts** Lydney Park Estate (weekends & school hols only) 01594 844841. Nailsworth: **Paint-a-Pot** 5 Cossack Sq 01453 835043.

WILTSHIRE: Salisbury: **Splash of Colour** 72 Fisherton St 01722 322250.

Swindon(near): **Studley Grange Craft Village,** Hay Lane, Wroughton, www.studleygrange.co.uk 01793 852400. A family day out that's full of interest and a great venue for birthday parties. There are hands-on craft activities, a café, Butterfly World (see 'Farms' chapter), Bonkers play area (see 'Adventure' chapter) and a portrait photographer. These options can be mixed and matched to design your own birthday celebration, not forgetting food in the café. Village open daily, 10am-6pm (dusk in Winter), but check times for individual attractions (see below). Birthdays **Open all year Price P Check out page 20.**

Ferris Photographics, 07765 197810, specialises in portraits of families, children and pets in a natural, contemporary style. Please telephone to discuss requirements.

Master Plaster Casters, 01793 855850, has a delightful variety of plaster models waiting to be painted (from £1.25, including materials). Plaster-casting kits for sale. Closed Mons in term time. Birthdays.

PeopleKraft Ltd, 01793 849372. Paint mugs, plates and bowls that are fully useable. All ages welcome. Create a precious memento with hand and foot ceramic imprints. Closed Mons in term time. Birthdays.

Snazzy Bear Originals, 01793 855377. Drop in and make cards or ring for a free timetable of workshops where you can try stamping, stencilling, papercraft, clockmaking and scrapbooking. Birthdays.

BRISTOL & BATH AREA: Bath(near): **Wellow Trekking Centre** Wellow (groups only) 01225 834376. Bristol: **West Country Mini Quads** Bradley Stoke 01454 202666. Churchill: **High Action Ltd** Lyncombe Dri 01934 852335. Weston-super-Mare: **Kidz Quadz** 0845 226 7476.

GLOUCESTERSHIRE: Lydney(near): **Wye Valley Quad Bikes Ltd** Tidenham 01291 689940. Moreton-in-Marsh: **Cotswold Paintballing and Quadbiking** 07836 657397.

WILTSHIRE: Chippenham: **Kiddie Pursuits** Lacock (groups only) 01249 730388.

Check with your local council for free facilities in parks.
BRISTOL & BATH AREA: Bristol: **Park Central** 74-8 Avon Street St Philips 0117 907 9995.
Churchill: **High Action Ltd** Lyncombe Dri 01934 852335.

SNOW SPORTS

BRISTOL & BATH AREA: Churchill: **Avon Ski Centre** Lyncombe Dri 01934 852335.
GLOUCESTERSHIRE: Gloucester: **Gloucester Ski & Snowboard Centre** Matson La 0870
240 0375.

SPECTATOR SPORTS

BRISTOL & BATH AREA: Bath: **Bath Rugby Club** The Recreation Ground Spring Gdns
01225 325200. Bristol: **Bristol City FC** Ashton Gate 0870 112 1897, **Bristol Rovers FC**
Memorial Ground Filton Ave 0117 909 6648, **Bristol Rugby Club** Memorial Stadium Filton Ave
0117 952 0500, **Gloucestershire County Cricket Club** County Ground Nevil Rd (also at
Gloucester and Cheltenham Cricket Festivals) 0117 910 8000.
GLOUCESTERSHIRE: Cheltenham: **Cheltenham Town FC** Whaddon Rd 01242 573558,
Prescott Speed Hill Climb Prescott Hill Gotherington 01242 673136. Gloucester: **Gloucester
Rugby Club** Kingsholm Stadium Kingsholm Rd 0871 871 8781.
WILTSHIRE: Castle Combe: **Castle Combe Circuit** 01249 782417. Swindon: **Swindon
Speedway** Abbey Stadium Blunsdon 01793 704127, **Swindon Town FC** County Rd 0870 443
1894, **Swindon Wildcats** (ice hockey) Link Centre Whitehill Way Westlea 01793 445566.

SPORTS & LEISURE CENTRES

Leisure departments at local councils have details of additional 'dual use' centres, used by schools
during the day, but open to the public in the evenings, at weekends and during school holidays.
* Centre has a swimming pool.
BRISTOL & BATH AREA: Backwell: **Backwell LC*** Farleigh Rd 01275 463726. Bath: **Bath
S&LC*** North Parade Rd 01225 462565, **Culverhay SC*** Rush Hill 01225 480882, **Sports
Training Village*** University of Bath 01225 386339. Bristol: **Bradley Stoke LC*** Fiddlers Wood
La 01454 867050, **Coombe Dingle Sports Complex** Coombe La 0117 962 6718, **Downend
SC** Garnett Pl 0117 956 0688, **Easton LC*** Thrissell St 0117 955 8840, **Filton S&LC*** (Dolphin
Pool) Elm Pk 01454 866696, **Horfield SC*** (pool due to open May 2005) Dorian Rd 0117 952
1650, **Kingsdown SC** Portland St 0117 942 6582, **Kingswood LC*** Church Rd Staple Hill 01454
865700, **Patchway SC** Hempton La 01454 865890, **Robin Cousins SC** off West Town Rd
Avonmouth 0117 982 3514, **St Paul's Community Sports Academy** Newfoundland Rd 0117
377 3405, **Whitchurch SC** Bamfield 01275 833911. Churchill: **Churchill SC*** Churchill Gr
01934 852303. Clevedon: **Strode LC*** Strode Rd 01275 879242. Keynsham: **Keynsham LC***
Temple St 01225 395161. Midsomer Norton: **South Wansdyke SC*** Rackvernal Rd 01761
415522. Nailsea: **Scotch Horn LC** Brockway 01275 856965. Portishead: **Parish Wharf LC***
Harbour Rd 01275 848494. Thornbury: **Thornbury LC*** Alveston Hill 01454 865777. Weston-
super-Mare: **Hutton Moor LC*** Hutton Moor Rd 01934 635347. Yate: **Yate LC*** Kennedy Way
01454 865800, **Yate Outdoor Sports Complex** behind Brimsham Green School 01454 865820.
GLOUCESTERSHIRE: Bourton-on-the-Water: **Bourton LC*** Station Rd 01451 824024.
Cheltenham: **Leisure@cheltenham*** Tommy Taylors La 01242 528764. Chipping
Campden: **Chipping Campden SC*** Cidermill La 01386 841595. Cinderford: **Heywood LC***
Causeway Rd 01594 824008. Cirencester: **Cotswold LC*** Tetbury Rd 01285 654057. Coleford:
Five Acres LC* Berry Hill 01594 835388. Dursley: **Dursley SC** Rednock Dri 01453 546441.
Gloucester: **Brockworth SC*** Mill La 01452 863518, **GL1 Gloucester LC*** Bruton Way 01452
396666, **Sir Thomas Rich's SC** Oakleaze Longlevens 01452 338439. Lydney: **Whitecross LC***

20

Church Rd 01594 842383. Newent: **Newent LC*** Watery La 01531 821519. Stroud: **Stratford Park LC*** Stratford Rd 01453 766771. Tetbury: **Tetbury S&LC*** (outdoor pool only) Sir William Romney School Lowfield Rd 01666 505805. Wotton-under-Edge: **Wotton SC** Kingswood Rd 01453 842626.

WILTSHIRE: Calne: **White Horse LC*** White Horse Way 01249 814032. Chippenham: **Olympiad LC*** Monkton Pk 01249 444144. Corsham: **Springfield SC*** Beechfield Rd 01249 712846. Cricklade: **Cricklade LC*** Stones La 01793 750011. Devizes: **Devizes LC*** Southbroom Rd 01380 728894. Downton: **Downton LC** Wick La 01725 513668. Highworth: **The Rec*** (an outdoor pool, but likely to be roofed over during 2005) **The Elms** 01793 762602. Malmesbury: **Activity Zone*** Bremilham Rd 01666 822533. Marlborough: **Marlborough LC*** Barton Dene 01672 513161. Melksham: **Christie Miller SC** 32 Lancaster Rd Bowerhill 01225 702826. Pewsey: **Pewsey SC*** Wilcot Rd 01672 562469. Salisbury: **Five Rivers LC*** The Butts Hulse Rd 01722 339966. Stratton: **Stratton Community LC** Grange Dri 01793 825525. Swindon: **Croft SC** Marlborough La Old Town 01793 526622, **Dorcan Recreation Complex*** St Paul's Dri Covingham 01793 533763, **Haydon Centre** Thames Ave Haydon Wick 01793 706666, **Link Centre*** Whitehill Way Westlea 01793 445566, **Oasis LC*** North Star Ave 01793 445401. Tidworth: **Tidworth LC*** Nadder Rd 01980 847140. Tisbury: **Tisbury & District SC** Weaveland Rd 01747 871141. Trowbridge: **Trowbridge SC*** Frome Rd 01225 764342. Warminster: **Warminster SC*** Woodcock Rd 01985 212946. Westbury: **Leighton RC** Wellhead La 01373 824448. Wootton Bassett: **Lime Kiln LC*** 01793 852197. Wroughton: **Ridgeway LC*** Inverary Rd 01793 813280.

South Gloucestershire Leisure Centres offer a wide variety of activities and organise exciting holiday programmes. Log onto www.southglos.gov.uk/whatson to keep up to date. **Check out inside back cover.**

SWIMMING POOLS (INDOOR)

Also see 'Sports & Leisure Centres' listing above. Those marked with an * have a pool.
BRISTOL & BATH AREA: Bristol: **Bishopsworth Pool** Whitchurch Rd 0117 964 0258, **Bristol North Pool** 98 Gloucester Rd Bishopston 0117 924 3548, **Bristol South Pool** Dean La Bedminster 0117 966 3131, **Filwood Swimming Pool** Filwood Broadway Knowle West 0117 966 2823, **Henbury Swimming Pool** Crow La 0117 950 0141, **Jubilee Pool** Jubilee Rd Knowle 0117 977 7900, **Shirehampton Pool** Park Rd 0117 982 2627, **Speedwell Pool** Whitefield Rd 0117 967 4778, **Winterbourne Swimming Pool** The Ridings High School Winterbourne 01454 252090. Paulton: **Swimming Pool** Plumptre Rd 01761 413644.
GLOUCESTERSHIRE: Dursley: **Dursley Swimming Pool** Castle St 01453 546441. Tewkesbury: **Cascades** Oldbury Rd 01684 293740.
WILTSHIRE: Bradford-on-Avon: **Bradford Pool** St Margaret's St 01225 862970. Durrington: **Durrington Swimming Pool** Recreation Rd 01980 594594. Melksham: **Blue Pool** Market Pl 01225 703525. Swindon: **Health Hydro** Milton Rd 01793 465630. Westbury: **Westbury Pool** Church St 01373 822891.

SWIMMING POOLS (OUTDOOR)

BRISTOL & BATH AREA: Portishead: **Open Air Pool** Esplanade Rd 01275 843454.
GLOUCESTERSHIRE: Cheltenham: **Sandford Parks Lido** Keynsham Rd 01242 524430. Cirencester: **Cirencester Open Air Swimming Pool** off Cecily Hill 01285 653947. Lydney: **Bathurst Outdoor Swimming Pool** 01594 842625. Stroud: **Stratford Park Leisure Centre** Stratford Rd 01453 766771. Tetbury: **Tetbury Sports & Leisure Centre** Sir William Romney School Lowfield Rd 01666 505805. Wotton-under-Edge: **Wotton Outdoor Pool** Symm La 01453 842626.
WILTSHIRE: Highworth: **The Rec Outdoor Pool** (likely to be roofed over during 2005) The Elms 01793 762602. Tisbury: **Tisbury Outdoor Pool** Weaveland Rd 01747 871180.

BRISTOL & BATH AREA: Bristol: **Coombe Dingle Sports Complex** Coombe La 0117 962 6718.
GLOUCESTERSHIRE: Gloucester: **Oxstalls Indoor Tennis Centre** Plock Court Tewkesbury Rd 01452 396969.
WILTSHIRE: Swindon: **Delta Tennis Centre** Welton Rd Westlea 01793 445555.

BRISTOL & BATH AREA: Bath: **Rondo Theatre** St Saviour's Rd Larkhall 01225 463362, **Theatre Royal Bath** Sawclose 01225 448844. Bristol: **Arnolfini** Narrow Quay (due to re-open summer 2005) 0117 917 2300, **Bristol Hippodrome** St Augustine's Pde 0870 607 7500, **Bristol Old Vic** King St 0117 987 7877, **Colston Hall** Colston St 0117 922 3683, **QEH Theatre** Jacob's Wells Rd 0117 930 3082, **Redgrave Theatre** Percival Rd Clifton 0117 315 7600, **Ridings Arts Centre** High St Winterbourne 0117 956 8812, **St George's Bristol** Great George St 0117 923 0359, **Tobacco Factory Theatre** Raleigh Rd Southville 0117 902 0344. Weston-super-Mare: **Playhouse Theatre** High St 01934 645544.
GLOUCESTERSHIRE: Cheltenham: **Bacon Theatre** Hatherley Rd 01242 258002, **Everyman Theatre** Regent St 01242 572573, **Playhouse Theatre** Bath Rd 01242 522852. Cirencester: **Brewery Arts** Brewery Court 01285 655522, **Sundial Theatre** Cirencester College 01285 654228. Coleford: **Forest Theatre** Royal Forest of Dean College Five Acres Campus Berry Hill 01594 833416. Gloucester: **Guildhall Arts Centre** 23 Eastgate St 01452 396370, **King's Theatre** Kingsbarton St 01452 300130, **New Olympus Theatre** 162-166 Barton St 01452 525917. Stroud: **Cotswold Playhouse** Parliament St 01453 756379. Tewkesbury: **Roses Theatre** Sun St 01684 295074. Uley: **Prema Arts Centre** South St 01453 860703.
WILTSHIRE: Devizes: **Wharf Theatre** 01380 725944. Salisbury: **Salisbury Arts Centre** Bedwin St 01722 321744, **Salisbury City Hall** Malthouse La 01722 434434, **Salisbury Playhouse** Malthouse La 01722 320333, **Studio Theatre** Ashley Rd 01722 338579. Swindon: **Swindon Arts Centre** Devizes Rd 01793 614837, **Wyvern Theatre** Theatre Sq 01793 524481. Trowbridge: **Arc Theatre** College Rd 01225 756376. Warminster: **Athenaeum Centre** High St 01985 213891.

BRISTOL & BATH AREA: Banwell: **Mendip Outdoor Pursuits** 01934 820518/823666 C K Rt. Bristol: **The Adventurous Activity Company** Hotwell Rd 0117 925 3196 C, **Bristol Activities Centre** Cumberland Basin 0117 926 5850 (groups only) C K, **Bristol Sailing School** Baltic Wharf Leisure Centre Cumberland Rd 0117 907 3019 S, **Young Bristol Outdoor Activity Centre** Pooles Wharf 0117 953 7921 (groups only) C K S.
GLOUCESTERSHIRE: Christchurch: **Forest Adventure Ltd** 01594 834661 (groups only) C K Rt. Cirencester(Cotswold Water Park): **Craig Cohoon Waterski School** 01285 713735 Ba Ri Wb WS, **South Cerney Outdoor Education Centre** 01285 860388 C K S Sn W, **Waterland Outdoor Pursuits** 01285 861202 C K S Rt W, **Watermark Club** 01285 860606 Ri Wb WS. Coleford: **Wyedean Canoe & Adventure Centre** 01594 833238 C K Rt. Tewkesbury(near): **Croft Farm Leisure and Water Park** Bredons Hardwick 01684 772321 C K Rt S W.

BRISTOL & BATH AREA: Bristol: **Jumicar,** Asda car park, Cribbs Causeway, www.jumicarbristol.co.uk 01454 250 219. Road safety instruction for children using real junior sized cars. Children from ages 6-12 will enjoy and benefit from learning and practicing the rules of the road. Please call for details.

Free Places

Don't miss out on the free entertainment available in this area. Included here are museums, city farms, parks and open spaces with no admission charges. However, there may be car parking charges, requests for donations and charges for schools or special activities. There are also ideas for activities that will cost nothing.

Canals have towpaths for walking and cycling (permit needed if using own bike), boat trips, angling and boat hire facilities. Telephone 01452 318000 or go to www.britishwaterways.co.uk to search for information on the **Kennet & Avon Canal, Gloucester & Sharpness Canal, Thames & Severn Canal** and the **Stroudwater Navigation**.

Cycle routes. There are lots of quieter roads and traffic-free routes such as woodland tracks, disused railway lines and canal towpaths. Try Sustrans www.nationalcyclenetwork.org.uk 0845 113 0065, the Forestry Commission www.forestry.gov.uk/cycling or British Waterways www.britishwaterways.co.uk 01452 318000 for some suggestions.

Long-distance paths provide opportunities for shorter walks and rides as well. In this area are three National Trails - the Cotswold Way (some steep ascents), the Thames Path, the Ridgeway – and other paths including the Severn, Gloucestershire and Macmillan Ways. Visit www.nationaltrail.co.uk or try local information centres for maps and guides.

The Royal Society for the Protection of Birds has several reserves in Gloucestershire and puts on events throughout the area. Log onto www.rspb.org.uk or telephone 01594 562852 (Gloucestershire) or 01392 432691 (Bristol, Bath and Wiltshire) for more information.

Wildlife Trusts in the area manage nature reserves (ideal for outings or picnics) and organise family events. Contact Avon Wildlife Trust www.avonwildlifetrust.org.uk 0117 917 7270, Gloucestershire Wildlife Trust www.gloucestershirewildlifetrust.co.uk 01452 383333 or Wiltshire Wildlife Trust www.wiltshirewildlife.org 01380 725670.

BRISTOL & BATH AREA

The Forest of Avon, www.forestofavon.org.uk 0117 953 2141, covers 221 square miles in and around the Bristol area. There are many opportunities for walking and cycling and an events programme. Leaflets are available or visit the excellent website. Schools **Open all year.**

Aust, Aust Wharf, Old Passage Road, off the A403. Good views of both Severn bridges from this quiet stretch of road leading to the old car ferry site and from the Severn Way long-distance path running alongside. The Severn Bridges Visitors' Centre (see 'History' chapter) is nearby at Severn Beach. **Open all year.**

Bath, Alice Park, at the junction of A46 and London Road. This park has a well-equipped circular sandpit in the fenced play area, tennis courts and a cycle track for under 7s. **Open all year.**
Free Walking Tours of Bath, starting from outside the Pump Room in Abbey Church Yard, www.thecityofbath.co.uk 01225 477411. A two-hour walk with a member of The Mayor's Corps of Honorary Guides. Walks start Sun-Fri, 10.30am & 2pm, Sat, 10.30am; also, May-Sept, Tues & Fri-Sat, 7pm. Schools **Open all year.**
Royal Victoria Park. The largest park in Bath. The huge fenced play area (busy at peak times) contains an excellent variety of play and climbing equipment. There is also a skatepark, lake with waterfowl, crazy golf, approach golf course and tennis courts. **Open all year.**
Victoria Art Gallery, Bridge Street, www.victoriagal.org.uk 01225 477233, houses sculpture, ceramics, glass and paintings. Art trolleys and quizzes for children. Open Tues-Fri, 10am-5.30pm, Sat, 10am-5pm, Sun, 2-5pm. Schools **Open all year.**

Blagdon, Blagdon Visitor Centre, Station Road, www.bristolwater.co.uk/leisure 0117 953 6470. Interactive displays and videos show how Bristol Water ensure our water supply. See the beam engine in action, feed the trout and follow a nature trail. Open Summer, Suns, 2-5pm, but please confirm. Schools.

Bristol, Ashton Court Estate, off A369 near the Suspension Bridge, 0117 963 9174, is 850 acres of parks and woodland with something for everyone: nature trails, two deerparks, pitch and putt, an orienteering course (maps available at golf kiosk), a demanding mountain biking trail and a miniature railway (Apr-Sept, certain dates only). Use the Bower Ashton entrance to reach the visitor centre. Major events may restrict access. **Open all year.**

Blaise Castle Estate, Henbury, car park off Kings Weston Road, 0117 950 5447. Four hundred acres of wood and parkland with a folly, paths, trails and very popular, well-equipped play areas catering for a wide age range. **Open all year.**

Blaise Castle House Museum, Henbury, www.bristol-city.gov.uk/museums 0117 903 9818. Set in beautiful parkland, the 18th century building contains everyday objects from the past. There are model trains, exquisite costumes, pots and pans and ancient lavatories. Open Sat-Wed, 10am-5pm. Schools **Open all year.**

Brandon Hill, off Jacob's Wells Road, is topped by the Cabot Tower from which you have a panoramic view of the city. There is a nature park with information boards, a variety of habitats and a children's playground. **Open all year.**

Bristol and Bath Railway Path, 0117 922 4325 (Avon Valley Partnership). Equally suited to cyclists and pedestrians, this 13-mile path is car free and level. There are access points along the route and attractions, including Bitton Railway Station. **Open all year.**

Bristol City Museum & Art Gallery, Queens Road, www.bristol-city.gov.uk/museums 0117 922 3571. Find everything from sea-dragons, the Bristol box kite and Egyptian tombs to mammals, shells of the south-west and art in this friendly museum. Open daily, 10am-5pm. Schools **Open all year.**

Bristol Industrial Museum, Princes Wharf, Wapping Road, www.bristol-city.gov.uk/museums 0117 925 1470, with a full-size mock-up of Concorde's flight deck and a very popular double-decker bus. Learn about Bristol's transport, printing and packaging industries and the transatlantic slave trade. The harbour steam railway and steam tug operate on certain dates from March to October. Open Sat-Wed, 10am-5pm. Schools **Open all year.**

Castle Park, close to the city centre, is set around the remains of a medieval castle. Children can explore the fenced 'castle' playground: find wooden animals, people and 'buildings' to climb. **Open all year.**

CREATE Centre, Smeaton Road, www.createcentre.co.uk 0117 925 0505, houses a thought-provoking recycling exhibition. Next door is an Ecohome of interest to older children. Open Mon-Fri, 9am-5pm (4.30pm Fri), Ecohome open 12noon-3pm only. Schools **Open all year.**

The Downs, Clifton, are a huge expanse of open space for walking, ball games and kite flying. There is a small play area near the Suspension Bridge. **Open all year.**

Georgian House, 7 Great George Street, www.bristol-city.gov.uk/museums 0117 921 1362. This sugar merchant's town house shows what life was like in Bristol 'upstairs and downstairs'. Don't miss the cold-water plunge bath. Open Sat-Wed, 10am-5pm. Schools **Open all year.**

Hengrove Play Park, off Hengrove Way, park at Leisure Park. Choose between the 11m-high play dome with suspended pathways, state-of-the-art wheels park, sand and water play areas and a large grassed space for ball games. Open Mon-Fri, 11am-7pm, Sat-Sun, 11am-6pm; closes at dusk if earlier. **Open all year.**

Lawrence Weston Community Farm, Saltmarsh Drive, 0117 938 1128, is home to pygmy goats, turkeys, rabbits, quail, chinchillas and smaller farm animals. There is a picnic site. Open Tues-Sun, 8.30am-5.30pm (4pm Winter). **Open all year.**

Leigh Woods, NT/Forestry Commission, Abbot's Leigh, car park off A369 Portishead to Bristol road, 0117 973 1645. There are trails (one suitable for pushchairs), a cycle track, nature reserve, ancient hill fort and spectacular views of the Avon Gorge. **Open all year.**

Oldbury Court Estate (Vassalls Park), off Fishponds Road. With the Frome Valley Walkway passing through it, this extensive park is ideal for walks and picnics. The fenced children's play area is large and well equipped. **Open all year.**

Open Spaces-At-Bristol, Anchor Road, Harbourside, www.at-bristol.org.uk 0845 345 1235. A series of squares and open spaces displaying public art with striking water and light features, sculptures and landscaping. Look out for the giant beetle! **Open all year.**

Red Lodge, Park Row, www.bristol-city.gov.uk/museums 0117 921 1360. See the inside of an Elizabethan house. Ask for details of the popular 'living history' days. Open Sat-Wed, 10am-5pm. Schools **Open all year.**

St George Park, off A420, Church Road. An extensive park with a large area devoted to roller-skating, skateboarding and BMX bikes. There are also tennis courts, a lake with ducks and a play area. **Open all year.**

St Werburghs City Farm, Watercress Road, 0117 942 8241, is tucked away only a 30-minute walk from the city centre. Meet pigs, goats, sheep, poultry and rabbits or play on the rustic adventure playground. Open daily, 9am-5pm (4pm Winter). **Open all year.**

Windmill Hill City Farm, Bedminster, www.windmillhillcityfarm.org.uk 0117 963 3252. Visit a working farm with nature conservation area and adventure playground. Open Tues-Sun, 9am-5pm or dusk if earlier. Schools Birthdays **Open all year.**

Chew Stoke, Chew Valley Lake, www.bristolwater.co.uk/leisure 0117 953 6470. A good choice for a day out with picnic areas, glorious views across the lake, two nature trails (one suitable for pushchairs), information centre, tea-shop and restaurant. **Open all year.**

Clevedon, Salthouse Fields, off Church Road. Close to the seafront with lots to do in summer: crazy golf, putting, tennis, small fenced play areas and at the height of the season only, a miniature railway, bouncy castle and donkeys. **Open all year.**

Keynsham(near), Willsbridge Mill Environmental Education Centre, off A431, www.avonwildlifetrust.org.uk 0117 932 6885. Get ideas for attracting wildlife to your own garden, explore the Wild Waste Garden and take brass rubbings from the plaques on the Heritage Sculpture Trail (bring crayons and paper). Schools **Open all year.**

Portishead, Lake Grounds. On the seafront, with a fenced children's playground, a boating lake, tennis courts and pitch and putt in summer. In high season there are donkeys and a bouncy castle. **Open all year.**

Thornbury, Mundy Playing Fields. A large open area with play equipment, football pitches, tennis courts and children's paddling pool. **Open all year.**

Thornbury & District Museum, Chapel Street, www.thornburymuseum.org.uk 01454 857774. A social history collection tells the story of Thornbury and the Lower Severn Vale. Open Tues-Fri, 1-4pm, Sat, 10am-4pm. Closed Bank Hols & four weeks at Christmas. Schools **Open all year.**

Tortworth, Leyhill Arts & Gardens, Leyhill, 01454 264345, has a pets corner, arboretum, shop and art exhibitions. Children must be accompanied by an adult at all times. Open Tues-Sun, 9am-4pm. **Open all year.**

Weston-super-Mare, Ashcombe Park, one mile from the town centre between Upper Bristol Road and Milton Road. There is a children's play area and tennis courts. Pitch and putt is planned for 2005. **Open all year.**

The Beach and Seafront. A traditional summer's day out at the seaside: donkey rides, deck chairs, candy floss, good sand for castles, a land train and a variety of amusements and attractions. Weston won a Seaside Award in 2004.

Weston Woods. Numerous paths, trails and an ancient hill fort in 360 acres of woodland on Worlebury Hill overlooking Weston. **Open all year.**

GLOUCESTERSHIRE

The Forest of Dean, www.forestry.gov.uk 01594 833057. In the far west of the county, between the rivers Severn and Wye, are some 30,000 acres of woodland to explore. There are numerous trails, tracks, cycle routes, nature reserves and picnic sites plus great facilities for adventure activities and a year-round programme of special events. Here are a few suggestions.

Beechenhurst Lodge, 01594 827357, off B4226, W of Speech House, has a café, play area, picnic area and information on the Forest and local attractions. Open Mar-Oct, daily, 10am-6pm; Nov-Dec & Feb, daily, 10am-5pm or dusk if earlier, Jan, Thurs-Sun only. **Open all year.**

The Family Cycle Trail, is a traffic-free waymarked route of 11 miles. Hire bikes or bring your own. The trail can be picked up at several points including Beechenhurst Lodge. **Open all year.**

The Forest of Dean Cycling Association Trail, starting from Pedalabikeaway Cycle Centre. A challenging three-mile trail suitable for experienced mountain bikers. **Open all year.**

Mallards Pike, about five miles from Blakeney, off B4431 to Parkend, is an idyllic lakeside site with ducks and picnic tables. There are paths, tracks and a running trail for the more energetic. **Open all year.**

The Sculpture Trail, starting from Beechenhurst Lodge. Find the giant fir cone and the giant's chair. Just a couple of the favourites dotted along the four-mile trail. **Open all year.**

Wenchford, off B4431 Blakeney to Parkend. A wooded picnic site with tables, barbeques, trails and a stream. Don't forget wellies if you're hoping to paddle. **Open all year.**

Geology Trails. The Gloucestershire Geoconservation Trust, www.glosgeotrust.org.uk 01452 864438, has published guides for various geology trails in the county. Sift through the spoil and see what fossils you can find. **Open all year.**

The Severn Bore, www.environment-agency.gov.uk 0870 850 6506, is a tidal wave that rushes up the river at certain times only. A timetable is available but the size cannot always be predicted accurately. This natural phenomenon can be spectacular but be sure to pick your viewing point (and parking place) with care, as the water level will rise!

Cheltenham, Cheltenham Art Gallery & Museum, Clarence Street, www.cheltenham.artgallery.museum 01242 237431. Well-planned displays cover local history. There is a small gallery devoted to Edward Wilson who died with Captain Scott and various activities for children. Open Mon-Sat, 10am-5.20pm. Closed Bank Hols. Schools **Open all year.**

Hall of Fame, Cheltenham Racecourse, www.cheltenham.co.uk 01242 513014. The story of steeplechasing and of some of its legends. Open Mon-Fri, 9am-5pm. Admission charge on racedays. Schools **Open all year.**

Pittville Park. A large attractive park adjacent to the impressive Pump Room. There are ornamental lakes and gardens, as well as a fenced children's play area, skatepark and aviaries. In summer there is tennis and approach golf. **Open all year.**

Wishing Fish Clock, Regent Arcade. Each half hour a crowd gathers to watch this intriguing clock spring into action. The monster fish blows bubbles - catch one and make a wish. **Open all year.**

Cheltenham(near), Crickley Hill Country Park, just off A436, four miles S of Cheltenham, 01452 863170. Over 140 acres of woodland and parkland on the edge of the Cotswold escarpment. There are the remains of an ancient hill fort, well-marked trails and a new geology trail (guide available from visitor centre, open Apr-Sept). Schools **Open all year.**

Cirencester, St Michael's Park, off King's Street. An attractive, well-kept park with two play areas: one for small children and the other a small, rustic adventure trail. There are also tennis courts, crazy golf and in summer, croquet, putting and barbecues for hire. **Open all year.**

Cirencester(near), Cotswold Water Park, www.waterpark.org 01285 861459, includes the Keynes Country Park with nature reserves, trails, café, children's beach, play areas, boat and cycle hire, picnic sites and high ropes course. A range of adventure activities and water sports are available in school holidays (pre-booking essential). Start your visit by calling in at the Gateway Centre (on B4696 Spine Road, just off A419). Schools **Open all year.**

Free Places**Gloucester, Gloucester Cathedral,** off Westgate Street, www.gloucestercathedral.uk.com 01452 528095. Find the tomb of Edward II and see where scenes from the Harry Potter films were shot. A free leaflet for children brings this Norman cathedral alive. Open daily, 9am-6pm; special events restrict access. Schools **Open all year.**

Gloucester City Museum and Art Gallery, Brunswick Road, 01452 396131. Dinosaurs, fossils, Roman remains, paintings, local wildlife, hands-on displays and interactive computers make this a very family-friendly museum. Open Tues-Sat, 10am-5pm. Schools **Open all year.**

Gloucester Folk Museum, 99-103 Westgate Street, 01452 396131. More than three floors on local history and crafts with computer quizzes and hands-on activities. Open most school hols, telephone for details. Schools.

Gloucester Park, Parkend Road, is undergoing major refurbishment. A fantastic new play area may be open by the middle of summer 2005. Meanwhile, this central park still has the skatepark, multi-play area and existing play equipment. **Open all year.**

Robinswood Hill Country Park, Reservoir Road, 01452 303206. Paths and a geology trail criss-cross 250 acres of countryside that is perfect for walks and picnics. On site are the Rare Breeds Farm and the Gloucestershire Wildlife Trust Conservation Centre. Schools **Open all year.**

St James City Farm, 23 Albany Street, Tredworth, 01452 305728, offers hands-on contact with a variety of farm animals. Telephone for opening times. Schools.

Westgate Leisure Area, St Oswalds Road, 01452 414100. There is a lake with rowing boats and canoes for hire, pitch and putt course, picnic benches and riverside walks. Open Easter-Sept.

Gloucester(near), Over Farm Market, on A40 to Highnam, www.over-farm-market.com 01452 521014, is home to a water buffalo, a fallow deer, donkeys, pot-bellied pigs and greedy goats (animal feed available). PYO fruit and themed trailer rides at certain times. Open Mon-Sat, 9am-6pm, Sun, 10am-6pm (5pm Winter). Schools **Open all year.**

Nailsworth(near), Coaley Peak Picnic Site, Nympsfield, on B4066, four miles SW of Stroud. Stretch your legs on a 12-acre site with lots of space, panoramic views of the Severn Vale, picnic tables, an ice-cream van (if you're lucky) and the remains of a long barrow. **Open all year.**

Stroud, The Museum in the Park, Stratford Park, 01453 763394, is full of imaginative displays - from dinosaur remains to the world's first lawnmower. Quiz trails and activity packs linking the museum to its parkland setting. Open Tues-Fri, 10am-5pm (4pm Oct-Mar), Sat-Sun, 11am-5pm (4.30pm Oct-Mar), & Bank Hols, 11am-5pm. Telephone for Dec times. Schools **Open all year.**

Stratford Park. A park with woodland walks, duck pond, bandstand, children's play area, skatepark, tennis courts and, in summer, putting. It adjoins the Leisure Centre and the Museum in the Park. **Open all year.**

Symonds Yat, right on the county border, has superb scenery, lovely riverside walks and from April to August you can watch the nesting peregrine falcons through powerful telescopes provided by the RSPB. See `Adventure' chapter. **Open all year.**

Tewkesbury, The Merchant's House (The Little Museum), 45 Church Street, 01684 297174. A restored medieval timber-framed house. Tudor 'living history' days for schools. Open Apr-Oct, Tues-Sat, Bank Hols, 10am-5pm. Telephone for Winter opening. Schools **Open all year.**

Tewkesbury Abbey, Church Street, www.tewkesburyabbey.org.uk 01684 850959, is an impressive building, larger than many cathedrals, with a leaflet and safari trail for children. Open daily, 8am-6pm; special events restrict access. Schools **Open all year.**

Wotton-under-Edge, Wotton Heritage Centre, The Chipping, www.wottonheritage.com 01453 521541. The small centre has information about this historic wool town and changing displays. Open Tues-Fri, 10am-1pm, 2-5pm (4pm Winter), Sat, 10am-1pm. **Open all year.**

WILTSHIRE

Avebury, Avebury Stone Circle, NT. The village is set within this famous stone circle. Walk around the stones for free and, to find out more, visit the Alexander Keiller Museum (admission charge, see 'History' chapter). Car parking outside the village. **Open all year.**

Bradford-on-Avon, Barton Farm Countryside Park. Set in a wooded valley and flanked by the river and the Kennet & Avon Canal, the park has plenty of walks and a path for cycling. A well-preserved 14th century Tithe Barn is maintained by English Heritage. **Open all year.**
Bradford-on-Avon Museum, Bridge Street, www.bradfordmuseum.com 01225 863280, displays the heritage of the region. The centrepiece is a rebuilt 120-year-old pharmacy shop. Quiz sheets are available. Please telephone for opening times. Schools **Open all year.**

Chippenham, Chippenham Museum and Heritage Centre, 10 Market Place, 01249 705020. Discover the town's rich heritage and listen to 'King Alfred' describing Saxon life and the struggle against the Vikings. Handling tables and a very popular model of a mill. Open Mon-Sat, 10am-4pm. Schools **Open all year.**
John Coles Park, Fleet Road. There are tennis courts, a fenced play area, bandstand, bowls and plenty of open space for games in this beautifully kept park. 'The Fun Day' (a free family event run by the town council) is held here on the first Sunday in August. **Open all year.**

Corsham, Corsham Tourist Information and Heritage Centre, Arnold House, 31 High Street, 01249 714660. Two child-friendly displays with touch-screen computers focus on the local woollen industry and stone quarrying. Open Mon-Sat, 10am-4.30pm; check Sat opening in Jan & Feb. Schools **Open all year.**

Devizes, Devizes Visitor Centre, Market Place, 01380 729408. A small interactive exhibition looks at Devizes Castle and the Civil War between King Stephen and the Empress Matilda. Open Mon-Sat, 9.30am-5pm. Schools **Open all year.**
Hillworth Park, off Queen's Road, has fenced play areas, space to run around, an aviary and tennis courts (walk on and play). **Open all year.**
Wadworth & Co Ltd, Northgate Brewery, www.wadworth.co.uk 01380 723361. On weekday mornings the majestic shire horses are usually to be seen working around the town and in the afternoons they are at home to visitors. Stables open Mon-Fri, 1.30-3.30pm. **Open all year.**

Devizes(near), Caen Hill Locks, off A361, W of Devizes. Walk along the towpath and discover how engineers were able to bring the Kennet & Avon Canal uphill to the town of Devizes. Visit before mid-afternoon and there may well be boats negotiating the locks. **Open all year.**

Malmesbury, Athelstan Museum, Town Hall, Cross Hayes, 01666 829258, has local history displays, coins, early bicycles and a fire pump. The children's corner has hands-on activities including brass and fossil rubbing. Telephone for opening times. Schools **Open all year.**

Marlborough(near), Savernake Forest, www.forestry.gov.uk 01594 833057. Once a royal hunting forest, there are 2,300 acres of woodland, rides, trails and open glades with deer still to be seen. The picnic site at Postern Hill (off A346 between Marlborough and Burbage) has barbeques for hire and information boards. **Open all year.**

Salisbury, Churchill Gardens, Southampton Road. A formal park with a lovely riverside walk. There is also a skatepark, roller hockey pitch and a fenced area with play equipment for younger children. **Open all year.**
Queen Elizabeth Gardens, Crane Bridge Road. Overlooking the Cathedral and water meadows, this attractive park has a good, fenced children's play area. **Open all year.**
Salisbury Cathedral, www.salisburycathedral.org.uk 01722 555120, is a medieval masterpiece. See an original Magna Carta, follow the children's trail looking for animals and symbols or take a guided tower tour (age/height restrictions apply). Donations expected. Open daily, 7.15am-6.15pm; special events restrict access. Schools **Open all year.**

Swindon, Coate Water Country Park, Marlborough Road, 01793 490150, surrounds a large fishing lake. There is pitch and putt, miniature golf, picnic and barbecue areas, play equipment, a nature reserve with bird hides and orienteering. In summer there is also a miniature railway (Sun & Bank Hol afternoons), a paddling pool and cycle hire. Schools **Open all year.**

Swindon Museum and Art Gallery, Bath Road, Old Town, 01793 466556, houses a collection of 20th century British art and displays of local history and archaeology. See the Egyptian mummy and find a huge crocodile. Open Mon-Sat, 10am-5pm, Sun, 2-5pm. Closed Bank Hols. Schools **Open all year.**

Swindon(near), Barbury Castle Country Park, Wroughton, 01793 490150. Dramatic scenery, a hillfort and other archaeological remains, picnic area and ancient trackways, including part of the Ridgeway National Trail. A glorious spot but exposed in bad weather. Schools **Open all year.**

The Great Western Community Forest, www.forestweb.org.uk 01793 466324. Explore the patchwork of woodlands, farmland, parks and open spaces that is developing around Swindon. The new paths and trails are ideal for family rambles – leaflets available. Events include community tree planting. **Open all year.**

Lydiard Park, Lydiard Tregoze, 01793 771419. Farmland and woodland walks, nature trails, a play area for children and a visitor centre with exhibitions. See Lydiard House in 'History' chapter. Schools **Open all year.**

Science Museum Wroughton, Wroughton Airfield, www.sciencemuseum.org.uk/wroughton 01793 846200, stores large objects such as aircraft, fire engines and cycles for the National Science Museum. Special events and open days throughout the year (only some are free admission). Schools.

Trowbridge, Southwick Country Park, just off A361, is still under development. There are picnic areas, footpaths, recently planted woods and arboretum plus a pond, information board and nature trails. **Open all year.**

Trowbridge Museum, The Shires, Court Street, www.trowbridgemuseum.co.uk 01225 751339, tells the story of a West Country woollen town. Look out for the Mouse Trail and excellent reconstructions of a weaver's cottage and Trowbridge Castle. Open Tues-Fri, 10am-4pm, Sat, 10am-5pm. Schools **Open all year.**

Trowbridge Park, Park Road, is West Wiltshire's largest park. It has a fenced play area and a hard court for volleyball, basketball, hockey and tennis. In summer there is crazy golf. **Open all year.**

Warminster, Lake Pleasure Grounds, off Weymouth Street. There is a large lake that is fed by the River Were, playground, skatepark, tennis courts, paddling pool and chip and putt in summer. **Open all year.**

Westbury(near), Bratton Camp and White Horse, EH, Bratton. Pack a picnic and enjoy the views from this Iron Age hill fort. Get close to one of the landmark white horses but take care as the surface, now concrete, is extremely slippery. **Open all year.**

In Association with
British Red Cross

If your child had a nosebleed...

1. Sit your child down with their head well forward. Ask them to breathe through their mouth. Then pinch their nostrils together for 10 minutes.
2. If the bleeding hasn't stopped, pinch again for 10 minutes then release the pressure. Repeat if necessary.

If the bleeding goes on for more than 30 minutes take your child to hospital.

For great kids fashion all year come to Adams Childrenswear.

Trips & Transport

Have a break from the family car. Join an organised trip or let children try out different forms of transport for themselves. You can hire boats or bikes, take bus tours, ride steam trains, cruise waterways or relax in horse-drawn carts.

BOAT HIRE

Narrow boats in this listing are available for day-hire.

BRISTOL & BATH AREA

Bath, Bath Boating Station, Forester Road, 01225 312900, canoes, punts and skiffs on the Avon. **Bath Narrowboats,** Sydney Wharf, Bathwick Hill, 01225 447276, narrow boats on the Kennet & Avon Canal.

Bathford, The Avondale Hotel and Waterside Restaurant, 01225 859847, canoes, a catamaran and rowing boats.

Bristol, Messing About on The River, Ferry Road, Hanham, 0117 947 5500, narrow boats.

Monkton Combe, Dundas Enterprises, Brassknocker Basin, 01225 722292, canadian canoes and self-drive electric boats on the Kennet & Avon Canal.

Portishead, Lake Grounds, off Esplanade Road, small craft including pedaloes.

GLOUCESTERSHIRE

Cirencester(near), Colin Mortimer Boat Hire, Lake 31, Keynes Country Park, Cotswold Water Park, 07970 419208, shuttle bikes, pedaloes, katakanus and rowing boats. **Waterland,** Keynes Country Park, Cotswold Water Park, 01285 861202, canoes, kayaks, sailing dinghies and windsurfing boards.

Gloucester, Westgate Leisure Area, St Oswalds Road, 01452 414100, canoes and rowing boats.

Lechlade, Cotswold Boat Hire, based at The Trout Inn, 01793 727083, day cruisers, rowing boats and self-drive electric boats on the Thames. **Riverside Boat Hire,** 01367 253599, day cruisers, motorboats, rowing boats and skiffs.

Slimbridge, Glevum Boat Hire, based at Slimbridge Boat Station, 01453 899190, narrow boats for cruising the Gloucester & Sharpness Canal.

Symonds Yat East, Wyedean Canoe and Adventure Centre, 01594 833238, canadian canoes and kayaks.

Tewkesbury(near), Croft Farm Leisure and Water Park, Bredons Hardwick, 01684 772321, canoes, pedaloes, sailing dinghies, surf bikes and windsurfing boards.

WILTSHIRE

Bradford-on-Avon, The Lock Inn, 01225 867187, canadian canoes and self-drive electric boats on the canal.

Devizes, Devizes Marina Ltd, 01380 725300, narrow boats.

Semington, Tranquil Boats, 01380 870654, self-drive electric boats on the Kennet & Avon Canal.

Trowbridge, Alvechurch Boat Centres, Hilperton Marina, 01225 765243, narrow boats.

BRISTOL & BATH AREA

Bath, Bath City Boat Trips, from Riverside/Pulteney Weir, 07980 335185. One-hour return trips downstream on the river with a commentary, Mar-Nov, daily. Charter trips also available. Schools **Price B.**

Bath Narrowboats, from Sydney Wharf, Bathwick Hill, www.bath-narrowboats.co.uk 01225 447276. Charter trips on the Kennet & Avon Canal. Schools Birthdays **Open all year.**

Bath Small Green Boat Company, from Riverside/Pulteney Weir, 01225 460831. Public and charter trips on the Avon in a small, wooden, electric 10-seater. Operates Mar-Nov. **Price A.**

Pulteney Cruisers, from Pulteney Bridge, www.bathboating.com 01225 312900. A trip on the Avon lasts about an hour. Operates daily, Spring-Autumn, weather permitting. Telephone for Winter times. Schools **Price B.**

Bristol, Bristol Ferry Boat Company, www.bristolferryboat.co.uk 0117 927 3416. Daily round-trip and waterbus services on the historic harbour. Stops include SS Great Britain and At-Bristol. Also charter trips. Schools **Open all year.**

The Bristol Packet, from SS Great Britain car park, www.bristolpacket.co.uk 0117 926 8157. Tours of the city docks with a commentary operate Sat-Sun and daily in school hols. Also private hire and cruises between Avonmouth and Bath. Schools **Open all year.**

Industrial Museum. Trips from outside the museum on special events days. See 'Free Places' chapter. **Price A/B.**

Messing About on The River, Ferry Road, Hanham, www.messingaboutontheriver.co.uk 0117 947 5500, run public trips, charter trips and Santa cruises on the Avon. Schools Birthdays **Open all year.**

Number Seven Boat Trips, 0117 929 3659. Hourlong trips with commentary and a ferryboat service (40-minute round trip) around the Floating Harbour at weekends and daily in school hols. Charter trips available. Schools Birthdays **Open all year.**

Waverley Excursions, from Cumberland Basin, www.waverleyexcursions.co.uk 0845 130 4647. Sail under the Suspension Bridge to Clevedon (this is a shorter one-way cruise) or to Devon and Wales in summer (round trips). Schools.

Clevedon, Waverley Excursions, from The Pier, www.waverleyexcursions.co.uk 0845 130 4647, operate summer cruises to a variety of locations. Look out for Junior Pirates Day! Also occasional sailings from Weston-super-Mare. Schools.

Monkton Combe, The Kennet & Avon Canal Trust, from Brassknocker Basin, www.bath-narrowboat-trips.co.uk 01749 850169. Public and charter canal boat trips run Easter-Oct. Schools Birthdays **Price B.**

Weston-super-Mare, The Kenneth Allsop Memorial Trust, from Knightstone Causeway, 01934 632307. Daylong trips to Steep Holm Island nature reserve, Apr-Oct. No under 5s. See 'Farms' chapter. **Price E.**

GLOUCESTERSHIRE

Cirencester(near), Cotswold Canals Trust, from Coates, www.cotswoldcanals.com 01285 643440. Sapperton Canal Tunnel boat trips are planned for Sundays in winter. Most suitable for 7 years and over. Please confirm before travelling. **Price A.**

Frampton on Severn(near), Cotswold Canals Trust, from Saul Junction, www.cotswoldcanals.com 01453 545042. Take a trip on the Gloucester & Sharpness Canal and look around the visitor centre. Operates Easter-Sept. Schools Birthdays **Price A.**

Gloucester, Gloucester Leisure Cruises, from Merchants Quay, www.nwm.org.uk 01452 318200. Canal trips, Easter-Oct. See National Waterways Museum in 'History' chapter and telephone for times. Schools Birthdays **Price A/B.**

Lechlade, Cotswold Canals Trust, from Riverside Park, www.cotswoldcanals.com 01446 760314. Public and charter trips on the Thames operate Spring-end Sept. Schools Birthdays Price A/B.
Cotswold River Cruises, from Halfpenny Bridge, www.rivercruises.co.uk 01793 574499. Public and charter trips on the Thames, Easter-Sept. Schools Price B.

Sharpness, Waverley Excursions, www.waverleyexcursions.co.uk 0845 130 4647. Occasional summer cruises to Somerset and the Devon coast (also from Lydney). Return by coach. Schools.

Symonds Yat East, Kingfisher Cruises, 01600 891063. Right on the county border there are 40-minute boat trips through the scenic Wye Valley. Operating daily, Mar-Oct, 11am-5pm. Schools Price B.

Symonds Yat West, Symonds Yat Leisure, 01600 890350. Trips run 10am-6pm. See 'Adventure' chapter.

Tewkesbury, Kingfisher Ferries, from Mill Street or Riverside Walk, www.telstarcruisers.co.uk 01684 294088. A ferry service on the Avon connects Tewkesbury and Twyning, Easter-Sept. Charter trips also available. Schools.

WILTSHIRE

Bradford-on-Avon, Kennet & Avon Canal Trust, from Upper Wharf, www.katrust.org 01225 868683. Public and charter trips along the canal, Easter-Oct. Schools Birthdays Price B.

Devizes, White Horse Boats, from The Wharf, www.whitehorseboats.co.uk 01380 728504. Trips on locally built narrow boats along the Kennet & Avon Canal, Easter-Sept. Schools Birthdays Price B.

BUS TRIPS

BRISTOL & BATH AREA

City Sightseeing, www.city-sightseeing.com. One of the most fun ways to see a town/city. Jump on an open-top double decker bus for a bird's eye view of the sights and fascinating commentary on England's interesting towns and cities. Hop on and off as often as you wish, tickets are valid for 24 hours (unless otherwise stated). Kids Club at selected locations. Call or visit the website to check operating dates, times and prices. Schools Price B (unless otherwise stated) **Check out page 35.**

Bath, The Bath Bus Tour, starting from Bus Station, www.firstgroup.com 01225 313222. Tickets on the multi-coloured open-top buses can be used for a whole day so there's plenty of time to stop off and explore. Tours operate Spring-mid Nov. Schools Price C.
Bath's Classic City Tour, starting from Terrace Walk, 07721 559686. Look out for these red and white open-top buses. This is a hop on/hop off tour with tickets valid for 24 hours. Buses run mid Jan-mid Dec. Schools Price B.
City Sightseeing, 01225 330444. Operates all year round. Tickets valid for two days. Price C.
Heritage City Guided Tours, 07836 742422, operate the Stonehenge Express coach tour (ticket includes fast-track admission to Stonehenge and discount on open-top bus tour of Bath). Schools **Open all year.**

Bristol, City Sightseeing, 01934 830050. Operates Apr-Sept.

Weston-super-Mare, First Bus, from Weston Pier, www.firstgroup.com 01934 416851. Take the bus to Sand Bay, a few miles up the coast. The round trip lasts about 50 minutes and buses (usually open-top) run Easter-end Sept. Price A.

BRISTOL & BATH AREA

Bristol, Bristol Bicycle Hire, Smeaton Road, 07803 651945.
Monkton Combe, Dundas Enterprises, Brassknocker Basin, 01225 722292.

GLOUCESTERSHIRE

Bibury, Bibury Trout Farm, 01285 740215.
Bourton-on-the-Water, Bourton Bikes, Lansdowne, 01451 824488. **Hartwells Cycle Hire,** High Street, 01451 820405.
Cirencester, Pedal Power, 5 Ashcroft Road, 01285 640505.
Cirencester(near), Go By Cycle, Lake 31, Keynes Country Park, Cotswold Water Park, 07970 419208.
Coleford, Pedalabikeaway Cycle Centre, Cannop Valley, 01594 860065.
Slimbridge, Slimbridge Boat Station, 01453 899190.
Stonehouse, Stonehouse Accessories, 18 High Street, 01453 822881.

WILTSHIRE

Bradford-on-Avon, The Lock Inn, 01225 867187.
Salisbury, Hayball Cycle Sport, 26-30 Winchester Street, 01722 411378.
Swindon, Coate Water Country Park, off Marlborough Road, 01793 490150.

HORSE & CART RIDES

BRISTOL & BATH AREA

Weston-super-Mare, A & A Carriages, 01934 820970. Climb aboard the wagonette for a 15-minute trip along the seafront. Trips run most days in summer, weather permitting. **Price A.**

WILTSHIRE

Salisbury, Wessex Horse Omnibus, from the Guildhall, 07718 046814. Rides around the city and through the river, Easter-late Autumn, Mon-Sat, from 10.30am (weather permitting). Pre-booking advisable. Birthdays **Price B.**

TRAIN TRIPS

National Rail Enquiries: **08457 48 49 50** **www.nationalrail.co.uk**

BRISTOL & BATH AREA

Bitton, Avon Valley Railway, www.avonvalleyrailway.co.uk 0117 932 7296 (24hr) or 0117 932 5538. One-hour journeys under steam with the option of stopping off at Riverside Station for a boat trip at certain times. Special events programme. Trains run Easter-Oct & also at Christmas. Site open daily. Telephone for details. Schools Birthdays.

Bristol, Industrial Museum. Short trips by steam train along the docks on special events days. See 'Free Places' chapter. **Price A.**

Weston-super-Mare, Weston Miniature Railway, Marine Parade, 01934 643510. Miniature narrow-gauge locomotives run for just over half a mile around the putting course and along the Beach Lawns. Open Spring Bank Hol-mid Sept, daily, from 10.30am, weather permitting. **Price A.**

GLOUCESTERSHIRE

Coleford(near), **Perrygrove Railway,** on the B4228, www.perrygrove.co.uk 01594 834991. Enjoy a trip on the 15" narrow-gauge steam railway, do the treasure hunt and explore the indoor village with its secret passages. Telephone for operating days. Pre-booking is essential for Christmas trains. Birthdays.

Lydney, **Dean Forest Railway,** Norchard Railway Centre, Forest Road, www.deanforestrailway.co.uk 01594 845840 or 843423 (24hr). Nostalgic trips by steam train or, occasionally, by diesel heritage multiple unit. Look out for special events. Open daily for static display. Trains operate Mar-Oct, & Santa specials run in Dec. Schools Birthdays.

Toddington, **Gloucestershire Warwickshire Railway,** www.gwsr.com 01242 621405. With the opening of Cheltenham Racecourse Station, the 'Friendly Line in the Cotswolds' now operates a round trip of 20 miles along part of the former Great Western main line. Special events for children include a 'Day out with Thomas' and be sure to catch a Santa Special in December (advance booking essential). A narrow-gauge steam railway runs alongside the main car park on selected weekends and there is an exhibition, gift shop and tearoom, you can also board at Winchcombe and Cheltenham Racecourse. Operates most weekends, & daily in some school hols. Schools Birthdays **Open all year Check out below.**

WILTSHIRE

Swindon(near), **Swindon & Cricklade Railway,** Blunsdon Station, between Swindon and Cricklade, off A419, www.swindon-cricklade-railway.org 01793 771615. Trips by steam on special events days and by diesel at other times. Restoration centre and old signal box. Trains operate, Suns, Bank Hol Mons & at other times for special events. Site also open Sats. Schools Birthdays **Open all year**.

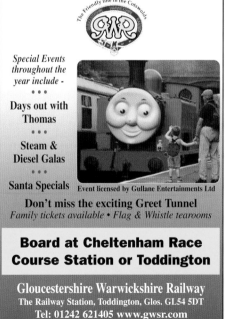

'If only I'd known what to do....'

In an emergency it's more likely to be someone you know who'll need your help. Whether it's your own child, a friend or a parent, not knowing what to do could ruin your day out or much worse.

The good news is it takes very little of your time to develop basic first aid skills that will make all the difference.

The brand new *5-Minute First Aid* series from the **British Red Cross** gives you all the essential first aid skills you need. Presented in five-minute sections, you'll build up your knowledge and confidence in no time.

Whether it's treating a cut or saving a life, make sure you have a safe day out.

What's stopping you?

There are six titles in the **5-Minute First Aid** series First Aid for Babies, First Aid for Children, First Aid for the Elderly, First Aid for Travel, First Aid for Sport and First Aid Life-Saving Skills.

The **5-Minute First Aid** series is available from all good bookshops and online retailers, priced £6.99 (from May 2005). For more information please call 020 7873 6481 or email:educationenquiries@hodder.co.uk

 # Learn First Aid

Would you know what to do if...?

... your child sustained a large burn at home?
One in five parents with young children would treat a child with a large burn incorrectly by applying things such as ice, butter or margarine to the injury.

... your child had a nasty fall?
Nearly a quarter of parents would not know what to do if their child fell and sustained a head injury, according to a survey published by the British Red Cross.

The British Red Cross offer a huge choice of ways to learn first aid, from the traditional course and books to interactive CD-ROMs or a DVD. You can learn as much as you want, when you want, where you want and how you want. It's convenient and easy to learn so there's no excuse!

- Watch a video or DVD in the comfort of your own home - 'Save a Life' £9.99
- Call your local Red Cross branch to find out about courses in your area
- Read the excellent '5 minute first aid for babies' and '5 minute first aid for children' each at £6.99 (see opposite).

Emergency First Aid Techniques

Assess the situation
- Keep calm and make the scene safe. Look out for any dangers to yourself or the casualty.
- Is there more than one injured child? Is there anyone that can help you?
- Do you need an ambulance?

Treat serious injuries first
- If more than one child is injured, go quickly to the quiet one, as they may be unconscious.

Resuscitation
- If the child is not breathing and there are no obvious signs of life, call for an ambulance.
- Pinch the child's nose, tilt the head back, place your mouth over the child's and blow. Deliver 2 rescue breaths.
- Give chest compressions. Place the heel of your hand on the child's breastbone and compress to one-third of the depth of the chest.
- Continue the cycle of one rescue breath followed by five compressions until emergency help arrives.

To find out more visit www.redcross.org.uk/firstaid,
call **08701 709222** or email firstaid@redcross.org.uk.
Details of the full range of products including a first aid kit for child carers are on the website.

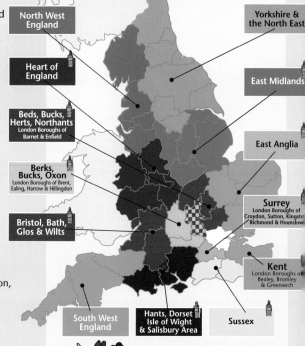

Plan a day out that is both educational and fun. This chapter includes castles, museums, cathedrals, art galleries, underground mines, a hands-on science centre and a windmill.

All these attractions have admission charges, but there are museums and places of interest that are free to visit. Check out the 'Free Places' chapter as well, so you don't miss anything.

Many of these sites and museums have exciting events programmes. Museums and art galleries run holiday activities and workshops or put on child-oriented exhibitions. There are jousts and battle re-enactments (even Easter Egg Hunts and Halloween Walks) at castles and other historic sites.

Guided Walks make an excellent introduction to a town or city. There is a wide range of themed walks to choose from, including a **Pirate Walk** in Bristol and **Ghost Walks** in Bath and Salisbury. Contact local Tourist Information Centres for details.

BRISTOL & BATH AREA

Banwell, The British Bear Collection, Banwell Castle, www.banwellcastle.co.uk 01934 822263. Teddy bears of all shapes, sizes and colours plus lots of information about the history of bear-making. Open Summer, daily, 11am-5pm, Winter, Sat-Sun. Schools **Open all year Price A.**

Bath, American Museum in Britain, Claverton Manor, www.americanmuseum.org 01225 460503. Furnished rooms show how Americans lived from the 17th to 19th centuries. There is a special guidebook for children and an Indian tepee and covered wagon to look out for in the gardens. Open 19th Mar-30th Oct, Tues-Sun, afternoons, and also for Christmas season. Schools **Price B.**

Bath Abbey Heritage Vaults, www.bathabbey.org 01225 422462, has artefacts and audio tapes describing the past of this ancient site. Children's quiz (and small prize). Open Mon-Sat, 10am-4pm. **Open all year Price A.**

Bath Aqua Theatre of Glass, 105-107 Walcot Street, www.bathaquaglass.com 01225 428146. Demonstrations of free glass-blowing and stained glass-making. It can get very hot here. Open Mon-Sat, regular demonstrations throughout the day. Schools **Open all year Price A.**

Bath Postal Museum, 8 Broad Street, www.bathpostalmuseum.org 01225 460333. Follow the history of written communication since 2000 BC with the help of videos, computer games and quiz sheets. Open Mon-Sat, 11am-5pm, but confirm Winter opening. Schools **Open all year Price A.**

Building of Bath Museum, The Paragon, www.bath-preservation-trust.org.uk 01225 333895, shows how the Georgians built and lived in the city. Touch-screen computer, Georgian playhouse and family trails. Open mid Feb-end Nov, Tues-Sun & Bank Hol Mons, 10.30am-5pm. Schools **Price A.**

Holburne Museum of Art, Great Pulteney Street, www.bath.ac.uk/holburne 01225 466669, runs a programme of art activities. This museum is based upon a personal collection: everything from porcelain to paintings. Open mid Jan-mid Dec, Tues-Sat, 10am-5pm, Sun, 11am-5pm; please confirm times. Schools **Open all year Price A.**

Jane Austen Centre, 40 Gay Street, www.janeausten.co.uk 01225 443000. Learn about the author, her family, life in Regency Bath and the locations which feature in her novels. Quiz sheets for children are available. Open Mon-Sat, 10am-5.30pm, Sun, 10.30am-5.30pm. Schools **Open all year Price B.**

Museum of Bath at Work, Julian Road, www.bath-at-work.org.uk 01225 318348. Enter the world of Victorian entrepreneur Mr Bowler and then discover other ways people have earned a living in Bath since Roman times. Open Easter-Oct, daily, 10.30am-5pm, Nov-Easter, Sat-Sun. Schools **Open all year Price A.**

Museum of Costume, Assembly Rooms, Bennett Street, www.museumofcostume.co.uk 01225 477785. Four hundred years of fashion come to life with displays of original dress and free audioguides. The exhibition 'Jane Austen: Film & Fashion' runs until the end of 2005. Open daily, 11am-last admission 4pm (5pm Mar-Oct). Free to BANES residents – contact for terms. Schools **Open all year   Price B/F.**

Museum of East Asian Art, 12 Bennett Street, 01225 464640. Have a go at origami, learn about the Chinese zodiac and check out the activity packs, dressing up boxes, family resource area and range of school holiday activities. Open Tues-Sat, 10am-5pm, Sun, 12noon-5pm. Schools **Open all year   Price A.**

No 1 Royal Crescent, www.bath-preservation-trust.org.uk 01225 428126, is a grand, fully furnished Georgian town house with a family trail. Ask to see the handling boxes and spot the poor turnspit dog in the kitchen. Open Feb-Nov, Tues-Sun, Bank Hol Mons, 10.30am-5pm (4pm Nov). Closed Good Fri. Schools **Price B.**

Roman Baths and Pump Room, Stall Street, www.romanbaths.co.uk 01225 477785. Explore the only hot spring baths in Britain, largely unchanged since Roman times. Plan your visit carefully as it is always busy. Personal audioguides and regular guided tours. Open daily, times vary. Free to BANES residents – contact for terms. Schools **Open all year   Price C/F.**

William Herschel Museum, 19 New King Street, www.bath-preservation-trust.org.uk 01225 446865/311342, houses a Star Vault astronomy auditorium and displays covering social history, science, astronomy and music. Family trails and audioguides. Open mid Jan-mid Dec, Mon-Tues & Thurs-Fri, 1-5pm, Sat-Sun, 11am-5pm. Schools **Open all year   Price A.**

Bath(near), Dyrham Park, NT, off A46, N of Bath, 0117 937 2501. This William and Mary house has tracker packs to keep children busy and the surrounding ancient parkland is ideal for picnics. Reduced admission for park only. House & garden open 23rd Mar-29th Oct, Fri-Tues, 12noon-4pm (5pm garden). Park open daily, all year, 11am-5.30pm or dusk if earlier. Schools **Price C.**

Bristol has several museums with free admission. Find their details in the 'Free Places' chapter.
At-Bristol, Anchor Road, Harbourside, www.at-bristol.org.uk 0845 345 1235, has three main attractions which can be visited separately or combination tickets are available. Price quoted is for admission to one attraction only. Schools Birthdays **Open all year   Price C.**

> **Explore-At-Bristol.** A comprehensive science centre, full of interactive displays and hands-on activities. The whole top floor has been refurbished for 2005. Build a bridge or try out the Human Hamster Wheel! Open daily, 10am-5pm (6pm Sat-Sun, school hols & Bank Hols).
>
> **Imax® Theatre-At-Bristol,** makes the audience feel part of the action with a screen which is four storeys high and digital surround sound. See schedules for film times.
>
> **Wildwalk-At-Bristol.** From fossils to conservation and from amazing plants to thousands of tiny live creatures, this exhibition will open your eyes to the natural world. Open daily, 10am-5pm (6pm Sat-Sun, school hols & Bank Hols).

Bristol Blue Glass, Whitby Road, Brislington, www.bristol-glass.co.uk 0117 972 0818. Admire the skill of free glass-blowers and maybe then blow a glass bubble yourself (extra charge). Guided tours at quarter past hour until last tour 3.15pm. Open Mon-Sat, 9am-5pm, Sun, 11am-4pm. Schools **Open all year   Price A.**

British Empire and Commonwealth Museum, Temple Meads, www.empiremuseum.co.uk 0117 925 4980, is an exciting, interactive museum with an extensive education programme. The exhibition Pow Wow (due to run until the autumn) is a 'must' with tales of pirates and early pioneers. Open daily, 10am-5pm. Schools **Open all year   Price B.**

Clifton Observatory and Cave, 0117 974 1242. Visit on a bright day to see the spectacular panorama outside projected onto a screen by the camera obscura. Down a long, narrow flight of steps is a cave and viewing platform (no under 4s). Open Summer, Mon-Fri, 11.30am-5pm, Sat-Sun, 10.30am-5pm; Winter, Sat-Sun, weather permitting. Schools **Open all year   Price A.**

Concorde at Filton, Filton, www.concordeatfilton.org.uk 0870 300 0578. Board Concorde 216 for a guided tour and find out more in the visitor centre afterwards. Suitable for over 5s only, pre-booking essential. Schools **Open all year   Price D/E.**

Kingswood Heritage Museum, Tower Lane, Warmley, 0117 932 3276, has lots to look at and discuss. See a Victorian kitchen and find out how children worked down the mines. Open May-Sept, Suns, 2-5pm, & Bank Hol Suns & Mons (includes grottoes), 11am-5pm. Telephone for additional opening. Schools **Open all year** Price A.
Pirate Walk, www.piratewalks.com, around Harbourside. A 90-minute educational walk around old pirate haunts. Schools Birthdays.
SS Great Britain, Great Western Dock, www.ss-great-britain.com 0117 926 0680. Brunel's great ship, the forerunner to all great passenger liners, is being restored to her original splendour. Included is admission to the Maritime Heritage Centre and, when moored on site, to the Matthew replica. Open daily, 10am-5.30pm (4.30pm Nov-Mar). Schools **Open all year** Price B.

Bristol(near), Severn Bridges Visitors' Centre, Severn Beach, www.onbridges.com 01454 633511. Facts and figures on the two Severn crossings. Suited to older children. Open Easter-end Sept, Sat-Sun & Bank Hols, 11am-4pm. Schools Price A.

Clevedon, Clevedon Court, NT, Tickenham Road, 01275 872257, is a 14th century manor house with a nursery rhyme trail, a special guidebook for slightly older children and a quiz/trail for teenagers. Open Easter Day-Sept, Wed-Thurs, Sun, Bank Hol Mons, 2-5pm. Schools Price B.

Nailsea(near), Tyntesfield, NT, Wraxall, 0870 458 4500 (information line). A spectacular mansion where conservation work is ongoing. Access is likely to be via two-hour guided tours in 2005 – pre-booking essential. Tours run Mar-early Nov. Please confirm all details.

Radstock, Radstock Museum, Waterloo Road, www.radstockmuseum.co.uk 01761 437722. Imagine life on the North Somerset Coalfield and see reconstructions of a coalface, schoolroom and shop. Open Feb-Nov, Tues-Fri, Sun & Bank Hol Mons, 2-5pm, Sat, 11am-5pm. Schools Price A.

Weston-super-Mare, Helicopter Museum, Locking Moor Road, www.helicoptermuseum.co.uk 01934 635227, has over 60 helicopters and autogyros. Themed play area and events programme including Open Cockpit Days and Helicopter Experience Flights. Call for opening times. Schools **Open all year** Price B.
Heritage Centre, Wadham Street, 01934 412144. Models, pictures and photographs tell the story of the town, the sea and the countryside. Open Mon-Sat, 10am-4.30pm. Closed Bank Hols. Schools **Open all year** Price A.
North Somerset Museum, Burlington Street, 01934 621028, is a lively local history museum. Visit Clara's Cottage, discover the area's wildlife and stamp your passport as you follow the trail. Open Mon-Sat, 10am-4.30pm. Schools **Open all year** Price A.

GLOUCESTERSHIRE

Berkeley, **Berkeley Castle,** www.berkeley-castle.com 01453 810332. High points for children will be the massive Norman keep with dungeon, the Great Hall and the cell where the unlucky Edward II was murdered. Open Apr-Sept, Tues-Sat & Bank Hol Mons, 11am-4pm, Sun, 2-5pm; Oct, Suns only. Schools Price C.
Jenner Museum, www.jennermuseum.com 01453 810631. Touch-screen computers help explain the basics of immunology. Open Apr-Sept, Tues-Sat & Bank Hol Mons, 12.30-5.30pm, Sun, 1-5.30pm; Oct, Suns only. Schools Price A.

Bibury, **Arlington Mill Museum,** www.arlingtonmill.com 01285 740368. Catch a glimpse of another way of life (or even the ghost) as you find out about milling and view the collection of artefacts. Open daily, 8am-6pm. Schools **Open all year** Price A.

Bourton-on-the-Water, **Cotswold Motoring Museum and Toy Collection,** www.cotswold-motor-museum.com 01451 821255. Intriguing for children and nostalgic for parents, this is a varied collection of cars, motorcycles, pedal cars and motoring memorabilia. Don't miss Brum, the TV star. Open Feb-Nov, daily, 10am-6pm. Schools Price A.

Perfumery Exhibition, Victoria Street, www.cotswold-perfumery.co.uk 01451 820698, explains the history and development of perfume. Allow enough time for the small quiz – fun for older children and not as easy as you'd expect. Open Mon-Sat, 9.30am-5pm, Sun, 10.30am-5pm. Schools **Open all year Price A.**

Broadway(near), Snowshill Manor, NT, 01386 852410 is home to an amazing collection, ranging from dolls houses to Japanese samurai armour. There are tracker packs for children to use in the gardens. Open 25th Mar-30th Oct, Thurs-Sun (also Weds from 2nd May & Bank Hol Mons). House, 12noon-5pm. Gardens, 11am-5pm. Schools **Price B.**

Cheltenham, Holst Birthplace Museum, 4 Clarence Road, www.holstmuseum.org.uk 01242 524846. Learn how the Victorians lived: from toys in the nursery upstairs to the kitchen and scullery downstairs. Open Feb-mid Dec, Tues-Sat, 10am-4pm. Schools **Price A.**

Cheltenham(near), Chedworth Roman Villa, NT, Yanworth, 8 miles SE of Cheltenham, 01242 890256. The remains of one of the best exposed Romano-British villas in Britain. See the ruins of this 1,600-year-old 'stately home' and imagine yourself back in the fourth century. Look at the surviving mosaics, the hypocausts (Roman underfloor central heating), water shrine and the many objects in the site museum, and get a flavour of life when Britain was part of the Roman Empire. There is an audio tour and programme of special events throughout the year. Open Mar-Nov, Tues-Sun & Bank Hol Mons. Please telephone for times. Schools **Price B Check out page 46.**

Cinderford(near), Dean Heritage Centre, Soudley, www.deanheritagemuseum.com 01594 824024/822170. A Victorian forester's cottage, complete with pigs, is one of numerous displays telling the story of the Forest of Dean. Try your hand at wood rubbing and visit the adventure playground. Open daily, 10am-5.30pm (4pm Winter). Schools **Open all year Price B.**

Cirencester, Corinium Museum, Park Street, www.cotswold.gov.uk/museum 01285 655611, has something to interest children at every turn, from dressing up as a Roman soldier to computer 'interactives'. Recently refurbished, this is an outstanding museum. Open Mon-Sat, 10am-5pm, Sun, 2-5pm. Schools **Open all year Price A.**

Cirencester(near), Bristol Aero Collection, Kemble Airfield (map available from gatehouse), www.bristolaero.com 0117 950 0908. Concorde's cabin, helicopters, jets, satellites and guided missiles are all stored in a disused hangar. Children must be supervised. Open Easter-end Oct, Suns & Mons, 10am-4pm. Schools **Price A.**

Coleford, Great Western Railway Museum, in main free car park, 01594 833569/832032. A small museum with model locomotives, one life-size static and a working signal box. Miniature train rides. Open Sats, 2.30-5pm. Schools Birthdays **Open all year Price A.**

Coleford(near), Cinderbury Iron Age Farm, www.cinderbury.co.uk - due to open during 2005. Please watch the website for details. Schools.

Clearwell Caves, www.clearwellcaves.com 01594 832535, is an extensive natural cave system which is still mined for its iron ore. See pick marks on the walls and learn about Free Mining. Open Mar-Oct, daily, 10am-5pm; Nov-Feb, Sat-Sun (daily, 1st-24th Dec, for 'Christmas Fantasy'). Schools Birthdays **Open all year Price B.**

Hopewell Colliery, Cannop Hill, 01594 810706. Borrow a hard hat and follow a miner underground. Above ground there are train rides and a small exhibition (free admission). Open Easter-Oct, daily, 10am-4pm (last tour 3.15pm), & for 'Christmas Underground'. Schools Birthdays **Price B.**

Gloucester, National Waterways Museum, Llanthony Warehouse, Gloucester Docks, www.nwm.org.uk 01452 318200. Modern interactive technology, working exhibits and hands-on displays are used to brilliant effect. This is the story of the waterways brought to life. Boat trips are available (see 'Trips' chapter). Open daily, 10am-5pm. Schools **Open all year Price B.**

Soldiers of Gloucestershire Museum, Custom House, The Docks, www.glosters.org.uk 01452 522682, describes the life and triumphs of the Glosters over the last 300 years. See what a First World War trench was like and try on a uniform. Open daily, 10am-5pm; closed Mons in Winter. Schools **Open all year Price B.**

Many Museums have FREE admission. Check out Free Places chapter

Gloucester(near), Nature in Art, Twigworth, www.nature-in-art.org.uk 0845 450 0233. After viewing the diverse art, try some animal brass rubbings and activities or visit the play area. Open Tues-Sun & Bank Hol Mons, 10am-5pm. Schools Birthdays **Open all year Price B.**

Moreton-in-Marsh, Wellington Aviation Museum, www.wellingtonaviation.org 01608 650323, is a small tribute museum full of RAF artefacts. In the garden is an entire tail section of a Wellington bomber. More suited to older children. Open Mar-Dec, Tues-Sun, 10am-12.30pm, 2-5pm; Jan-Feb, Sat-Sun. **Open all year Price A.**

Nailsworth(near), Woodchester Mansion, Nympsfield, four miles SW of Stroud, off the B4066, www.woodchestermansion.org.uk 0800 970 7223. This beautiful mansion was abandoned before completion. Find doors that will always lead nowhere and watch the bats on live CCTV. Open Easter-end Sept, Suns and 1st Sat every month (every Sat, Jul-Aug), Bank Hol weekends (Sat-Mon), 11am-last tour 4pm. Schools **Price A/B.**

Newent, The Shambles Victorian Village, Church Street, 01531 822144. Enter a small Victorian country town. Spot the glass eyes in the taxidermist's shop! Open Mar-Oct, Tues-Sun & Bank Hol Mons, 10am-5pm or dusk if earlier, Nov-Dec, Sat-Sun. **Price B.**

Northleach, Keith Harding's World of Mechanical Music, High Street, www.mechanicalmusic.co.uk 01451 860181, has an amazing collection of self-playing musical instruments, beautiful clocks, musical boxes and automata. Join a tour, then watch and listen. Open daily, 10am-6pm. Schools **Open all year Price B.**

Northleach(near), Lodge Park & the Sherborne Estate, NT, Sherborne, 01451 844130. Find out what this 17th century grandstand was used for and even go up on the roof. Across the A40 is the Ewepen carpark, the starting point for the family walks around the estate (pick up a leaflet from the barn). Lodge Park open Mar-Oct, Fri-Mon, 11am-4pm (3pm Sat). Estate open all year, free admission. Schools **Price B/F.**

Stow-on-the-Wold, Toy Museum, Park Street, www.thetoymuseum.co.uk 01451 830159. Three rooms full of Edwardian, Victorian and later toys: dolls, teddy bears, trains and more. Open Feb-Apr & Jun-Oct, Wed-Sat, 10am-1pm, 2-4.30pm. Schools **Price A.**

Tewkesbury, The John Moore Countryside Museum, 41 Church Street, 01684 297174, is where you can learn about conservation and British wildlife with the help of a wonderful collection of preserved mammals and birds. Open Apr-Oct, Tues-Sat & Bank Hol Mons, 10am-1pm, 2-5pm. Telephone for Winter opening. Schools **Open all year Price A.**

Tewkesbury Museum, 64 Barton Street, 01684 292901. Study the model of the Battle of Tewkesbury or attend a 'living history' day at this small, friendly museum. Open Weds & Sats, 10am-4pm; phone for additional times. Schools **Open all year Price A.**

Winchcombe, Folk and Police Museum, Old Town Hall, www.winchcombemuseum.org.uk 01242 609151, houses a collection of police uniform and equipment from around the world and displays on local heritage. Ask for a free activity sheet. Open Apr-Oct, Mon-Sat, 10am-4.30pm. Schools **Price A.**

Sudeley Castle, www.sudeleycastle.co.uk 01242 602308. Queen Katherine Parr's tomb, a pheasantry and wildfowl area, glorious gardens and an adventure playground are highlights. Open daily, 19th Mar-30th Oct. Castle, 11am-5pm. Gardens & grounds, 10.30am-5.30pm. Gardens & grounds only, open from 26th Feb. Check website for prices. Schools

Winchcombe Railway Museum, Gloucester Street, 01242 602257. Try being a signalman or clip your own ticket in the booking office! This is a hands-on museum set within a half-acre garden. Open Easter-Oct, Wed-Sun, 1.30-4pm (5pm Sat-Sun), & daily in Aug. Schools **Price A.**

Winchcombe(near), Hailes Abbey, EH, off B4362, 01242 602398. Older children and adults can take a free self-guided audio tour around the atmospheric ruins of this 13th century abbey while younger children simply explore. Open 24th Mar-31st Oct, daily from 10am, closing times vary. Schools **Price A.**

WILTSHIRE

Amesbury(near), Stonehenge, EH, 0870 333 1181. Perpetual mystery surrounds these famous stones on Salisbury Plain. Open daily, times vary; check availability around summer solstice. Schools **Open all year Price B.**

Avebury, Alexander Keiller Museum, NT, 01672 539250, describes how Neolithic man lived in the area. Displays include tools and skeletons from the period. Ticket covers admission to an interactive exhibition in the Barn Gallery. Open daily, 10am-6pm (4pm Nov-Mar). Schools **Open all year Price A/B.**

Calne, Atwell-Wilson Motor Museum Trust, Stockley Lane, www.atwellwilson.org.uk 01249 813119. Many famous names of motoring in this collection of vintage and classic cars, quite a few are still in use. There is also a grass play area with traditional equipment. Open Sun-Thurs & Good Fri, 11am-5pm (4pm Nov-Mar). Schools **Open all year Price A.**

Calne(near), Bowood House, Gardens and Adventure Playground, www.bowood.org 01249 812102. A magnificent 18th century house with elegant rooms containing a wonderful collection of family heirlooms, built up over 250 years. These include paintings, porcelain, silver and such treasures as Queen Victoria's wedding chair, Napoleon's death mask, Lord Byron's Albanian soldier's costume and much more. Interesting rooms include Robert Adam's famous library, Dr Joseph Priestley's laboratory where he discovered oxygen gas in 1774 and the chapel. The surrounding pleasure grounds have lots to interest children including an extensive Adventure Playground and Soft Play Palace. Open daily, 19th Mar-1st Nov, 11am-6pm or dusk if earlier. Schools Birthdays **Price B/C Check out 'Adventure' chapter and page 10.**

Chippenham(near), Fox Talbot Museum of Photography and Lacock Abbey, NT, Lacock, 01249 730459. The museum commemorates the life and work of the 'Father of Modern Photography' and the abbey cloisters were used as a location in the Harry Potter films. Opening times and admission prices vary. Schools.

Crofton, Crofton Beam Engines, beside the Kennet & Avon Canal, SE of Marlborough, www.croftonbeamengines.org 01672 870300. The pumping station houses two early beam engines. Open Easter-Sept, daily, 10.30am-5pm. Please telephone for Steam Days. Schools **Price A.**

Devizes, Kennet & Avon Canal Trust Museum, The Wharf, www.katrust.org 01380 721279, is a fascinating exhibition with interactive video displays and models showing how the canal was built and used. Open Mar-mid Dec, daily, 10am-5pm (4pm Winter). Schools **Price A.**
Wiltshire Heritage Museum, 41 Long Street, www.wiltshireheritage.org.uk 01380 727369. See collections of archaeology, social and natural history, and art. Leave time for hands-on activities including brass rubbing and dressing up. Open Mon-Sat, 10am-5pm, Sun, 12noon-4pm; check Bank Hol opening. Free admission on Mons & Suns. Schools **Open all year Price A/F.**

Salisbury, Discover Salisbury, at The Medieval Hall, The Close, www.medieval-hall.co.uk 01722 324731. The big-screen presentation lasts 40 minutes and describes Salisbury past and present. Open to groups. Telephone for details. Schools.

Mompesson House, NT, The Close, 01722 335659, is an early 18th century house with beautiful interiors, a children's guidebook and an Easter quiz. Open 19th Mar-30th Oct, Sat-Wed, 11am-5pm. Schools **Price B.**

Old Sarum Castle, EH, www.english-heritage.org.uk/oldsarum 01722 335398. Originally a huge Iron Age hill fort, the ruins leave plenty of room for the imagination. Go to the excellent Kids' Zone on the website before you visit. Open daily, times vary. Schools **Open all year Price A.**

Redcoats in the Wardrobe Military Museum, 58 The Close, www.thewardrobe.org.uk 01722 419419, houses the Berkshire and Wiltshire regimental collections. Heroic exploits to learn about and a Redcoats Mission quiz sheet to complete. Open Apr-Oct, daily, 10am-5pm; Nov-early Dec & early Feb-Mar, Tues-Sun. Schools **Price A.**

Salisbury and South Wiltshire Museum, The King's House, 65 The Close, www.salisburymuseum.org.uk 01722 332151. Imaginative displays cover prehistory, Old Sarum, Romans, Saxons and local history. Try out the interactive exhibits in the Stonehenge Gallery. Open Mon-Sat, 10am-5pm, & Jul-Aug only, Suns, 2-5pm. Schools **Open all year Price A.**

Stourton, Stourhead House and Garden, NT, 01747 841152. Outside there are landscaped gardens with temples, grottoes and lakes just waiting to be explored. Inside, discover an elegant Palladian house. House open 18th Mar-31st Oct, Fri-Tues, 11am-5pm. Garden open all year, daily, 9am-7pm or dusk if earlier. Ticket price is for House and Garden. Schools **Price C.**

Swindon, STEAM - Museum of the Great Western Railway, Kemble Drive, www.steam-museum.org.uk 01793 466646. What was life like in the age of steam? Film footage, hands-on displays, reconstructions and locomotives recreate the past. Open Mon-Sat, 10am-5pm, Sun, 11am-5pm. Schools Birthdays **Open all year Price B.**

Swindon(near), Lydiard House and Park, Lydiard Tregoze, 01793 770401. Audio commentaries and re-created rooms bring this ancestral home alive. There is a quiz and teddy bear trail. Outside is a beautiful park (see 'Free Places' chapter). Open Mon-Sat, 10am-5pm, Sun, 2-5pm, (4pm Winter). House closes 1pm on second Sat in May. Schools **Open all year Price A.**

Tisbury(near), Old Wardour Castle, EH, 01747 870487. A picture-book setting with plenty of scope for pretend play. This is a family-friendly site with information panels and a free children's leaflet. Open end Mar-Oct, daily from 10am, closing times vary; Nov-end Mar, Sat-Sun, 10am-4pm. Schools **Open all year Price A.**

Warminster, Longleat House, off A36, on A362 Warminster to Frome road, www.longleat.co.uk 01985 844400. Widely regarded as one of the most beautiful stately homes open to the public and an excellent example of Elizabethan architecture, Longleat House is home to the 7th Marquess of Bath. Substantially completed by 1580, the House incorporates many treasures including fine French tapestries, exquisite ceilings and paintings. The Longleat Passport also includes access to Longleat Safari Park and many more attractions. House open Easter-end Sept, daily, 10am-5.30pm (guided tours available 10-11am), and for the rest of the year, 11am-3pm (guided tours only); closed 25th Dec. Please telephone to confirm tour details. All attractions open daily, 12th Feb-6th Nov. Schools **Open all year Price G Check out 'Farms' chapter and page 50.**

Wilton(near Pewsey), Wilton Windmill, off A338, E of Pewsey, www.wiltonwindmill.co.uk 01672 870202. Watch the video and join a guided tour. Climb the steep staircases and learn how a windmill works. Open Easter-Sept, Suns & Bank Hol Mons, 2-5pm. Schools **Price A.**

Wilton(near Salisbury), The Wilton Carpet Factory, King Street, www.wiltoncarpets.com 01722 742890. Tour a working factory, see the looms in action and find out how carpets are made. Tours run Easter-Oct, telephone for further information. Schools.

Wilton House, www.wiltonhouse.com 01722 746729, has 460 years of history. In the Old Riding School are the re-created Tudor Kitchen and Victorian Laundry. Quiz sheets, landscaped parkland and a massive adventure playground. Open 24th Mar-30th Oct, daily, 10.30am-5.30pm. House (only) closed Sats, but open Bank Hol weekends. Schools **Price C.**

Children are fascinated by the natural world. Whether you are looking for minibeasts, tigers, friendly farm animals, birds of prey, sea horses or flamingos, this chapter can point you in the right direction. Some beautiful gardens and arboreta are also included.

The places listed here have admission charges, but there are nature reserves and open spaces that are free to visit, so check the 'Free Places' chapter as well.

BRISTOL & BATH AREA

Banwell, Court Farm Country Park, www.courtfarmcountrypark.co.uk 01934 822383, has animals to stroke, cuddle and feed as well as great adventure play facilities. **Check out 'Adventure' chapter and page 10.**

Bath, Prior Park Landscape Garden, NT, Ralph Allen Drive, 01225 833422 or 0900 133 5242 (information line). This lovely garden has a Palladian bridge, fish lakes, fine views and a programme of family events. Sturdy shoes recommended. The car park is for disabled visitors only. Open Feb-Nov, Wed-Mon, 11am-5.30pm or dusk if earlier; Dec-Jan, Fri-Sun. Schools **Open all year Price B.**

Bath(near), Norwood Farm, Norton St Philip, www.norwoodfarm.co.uk 01373 834356, is a working organic farm with native rare breeds of cattle, goats and sheep. There are farm walks and a play area. A lovely opportunity to see lambing in spring. Telephone for opening times. Schools Birthdays **Price B.**

Bristol, Bristol Zoo Gardens, Clifton, www.bristolzoo.org.uk 0117 973 8951, has been voted 'Zoo of the Year 2004' by the Good Britain Guide. From the smallest and rarest tortoise in the world to the largest ape, there are over 300 exotic and endangered species. Enjoy a whole day filled with excitement and discovery. Visit Zona Brazil and meet the stunning and diverse species of the threatened coastal rainforests. Encounter stunning birds, grazing tapirs, endangered tamarins and the world's largest living rodent – the capybara. Award-winning Seal & Penguin Coasts with fantastic underwater viewing is a must for all visitors. Other favourites include Bug World, Twilight World, the Monkey House, the Reptile House and Gorilla Island. Open daily, 9am-5.30pm (4.30pm in Winter). Schools **Open all year Price C Check out page 46.**

HorseWorld, Staunton Lane, Whitchurch, off the A37, www.horseworld.org.uk 01275 540173. Visit HorseWorld and enjoy a great day out for all the family. Meet the friendly horses, donkeys and farmyard animals and learn about the rescue, rehabilitation and re-homing work. There's lots to see and do with 'touch & groom' areas, pony rides, live shows, tractor tours, museums and a video theatre, indoor and outdoor play areas, drop slides, nature trail and restaurant. Family events are organised throughout the year. An excellent venue for school trips, group visits and birthday parties. Every visit helps support the charity's work. Open Easter-Sept, daily, 10am-5pm; Oct-Easter, Tues-Sun, & daily in school hols, 10am-4pm. Schools Birthdays **Open all year Price B Check out page 46.**

Wildwalk-At-Bristol, Anchor Road, Harbourside, www.at-bristol.org.uk 0845 345 1235. Part of the At-Bristol complex, this is a stunning exhibition of the natural world. See `History' chapter.

Bristol(near), Noah's Ark Zoo Farm, Failand Road, Wraxall, between Bristol and Clevedon on the B3128, www.noahsarkzoofarm.co.uk 01275 852606, is home to 80 different species of animal. Find yourself face to face with camels, wallabies, rheas, geckos, bison, snakes and some enormous newcomers, the rhinos. There is lots of hands-on activity with animals to feed, chicks to hold and guinea pigs to cuddle. As well as these delightful residents, there are fantastic indoor and outdoor adventure play areas, tractor rides, animal shows and exhibitions, a hedge maze, café and shop. Open 12th Feb-29th Oct, Tues-Sat, 10.30am-5pm, & also Mons in school hols. Schools Birthdays **Price C Check out page 50.**

Weston-super-Mare, SeaQuarium, Marine Parade, www.seaquarium.co.uk 01934 641603. Touchpools, a dramatic underwater tunnel and the variety of environments will interest all ages. Follow the Discovery Trail and win a prize. Open Summer, daily, 10am-5pm. Telephone for Winter opening. Schools **Open all year Price B.**

Weston-super-Mare(near), Steep Holm Island, about five miles offshore, is run by the Kenneth Allsop Trust as a wildlife sanctuary. Boat trips can be made to the island from April to October. See 'Trips' chapter. **Price E.**

GLOUCESTERSHIRE

Arlingham, St Augustine's Farm, go straight through village and car park is on right, 01452 740277. Put on your wellies, watch the afternoon milking and feed the calves. Telephone for opening times. Schools Birthdays **Price A/B.**

Berkeley, Butterfly Farm, Berkeley Castle, 01453 810332. Admire the tropical butterflies fluttering around you. Open Apr-Sept, Tues-Sat & Bank Hol Mons, 11am-4pm, Sun, 2-5pm. Schools **Price A.**

Bibury, Bibury Trout Farm, 01285 740215. Learn about rainbow trout and try pond-dipping. Visit the play area and test your skill at the catch-your-own fishery (check opening). Open Summer, Mon-Sat, 9am-6pm, Sun, 10am-6pm; Winter, daily, 10am-4pm. Schools Birthdays **Open all year Price A.**

Bourton-on-the-Water, Birdland, Rissington Road, www.birdland.co.uk 01451 820480, is home to over 500 birds in a natural setting of woodland, river and gardens. Flamingos, pelicans, penguins and storks can be seen in water habitats and parrots, hornbills, toucans and many more birds are housed in the aviaries. The more delicate species can be found in the Tropical and Desert Houses. Don't miss Penguin Feeding Time which is always a particular favourite with children! Call in at the information centre to learn more about birds and to keep up to date with Birdland's latest news. There is a children's playground, a café and a gift shop. Bird of Prey Encounter Days are held during the summer and a Bird Adoption scheme is now in operation. Educational sheets are available. Open daily, Apr-Oct, 10am-6pm, Nov-Mar, 10am-4pm. Schools **Open all year Price B Check out page 48.**

Cirencester(near), The Butts Farm, South Cerney, 01285 862205. A family-run farm that is truly hands-on. Feed and cuddle the animals, visit the play area and take part in the daily activities, collecting stickers as you go. Open Feb half term-Oct half term, Tues-Sun, 11am-5pm. Schools Birthdays **Price B.**

Gloucester, Barn Owl Centre, The Tithe Barn, Brockworth Court, www.barnowl.co.uk 01452 865999. This small, friendly centre cares for birds of prey, both wild and those bred in captivity. Hands-on flying experiences can be arranged. Open Sat, 10am-5pm, Sun, 12noon-5pm, & daily in school hols. Schools Birthdays **Open all year Price A.**

Gloucester(near), Prinknash Bird & Deer Park, Cranham, www.prinknash-bird-and-deerpark.com 01452 812727. Hand-feed peacocks, waterfowl and fallow deer in this beautiful park or throw food to the trout. Open daily, 10am-5pm (4pm Winter). Closed Good Fri. Schools **Open all year Price B.**

Check out the Free Places chapter
for more wildlife and nature parks.

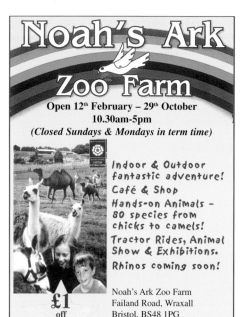
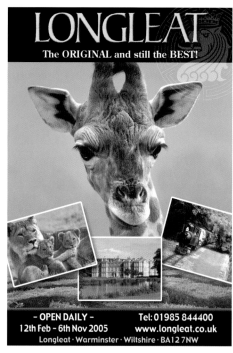

Guiting Power, **Cotswold Farm Park,** www.cotswoldfarmpark.co.uk 01451 850307, specialises in rare breeds. There are demonstrations, a touch barn, pets corner, adventure playground and mini 'Tractor Driving School'. Open 19th Mar-4th Sept, daily, 10.30am-5pm; 5th Sept-end Oct, Sat-Sun, & daily in Oct half term, 10.30am-4pm. Schools Birthdays **Price B.**

Moreton-in-Marsh(near), **Batsford Arboretum,** Batsford Park, www.batsarb.co.uk 01386 701441, has a children's trail and, in August, the Golden Pine Cone Challenge. Open early Feb-mid Nov, daily, 10am-5pm; mid Nov-early Feb, Sat-Sun, 10am-4pm. Schools **Open all year** Price B. **Cotswold Falconry Centre,** Batsford Park, www.cotswold-falconry.co.uk 01386 701043, has four flying displays daily, featuring eagles, hawks, falcons and owls. There is a new 'Owl Parliament' for 2005. Open mid Feb-mid Nov, daily, 10.30am-5.30pm. Schools Birthdays **Price B.**

Newent(near), **National Birds of Prey Centre,** signposted from Newent, www.nbpc.co.uk 0870 990 1992. A marvellous opportunity to observe and learn about all birds of prey. Wander around extensive aviaries to view these captivating creatures at close quarters. Admire eagles, vultures, falcons, buzzards, lots of owls and, if you're lucky, young birds as well. Informative and highly entertaining flying displays are held daily. There is a coffee shop, a gift shop and a new pets corner with rabbits, guinea pigs, gerbils, aquarium fish, stick insects and grass snakes. The Junior Raptor Club operates for 10-16 year olds. Open daily, Feb-Oct, 10.30am-5.30pm. Schools Birthdays **Price B Check out page 50.**

Painswick(near), **Painswick Rococo Garden,** www.rococogarden.co.uk 01452 813204, has a young privet maze, nature trail and striking architecture to intrigue children. See drifts of snowdrops in February. Open 10th Jan-end Oct, daily, 11am-5pm. Schools **Price B.**

Slimbridge, **Slimbridge Wetlands Centre, Wildfowl & Wetlands Trust,** off M5 between Bristol and Gloucester, www.wwt.org.uk 01453 891900, is an internationally important reserve and home to the world's largest collection of rare and exotic water-birds. A fun day out that's also educational. See beautiful ducklings in spring, migratory flocks of geese and swans in winter and flamingos all the year round. Feed some of the birds and call in at the Discovery Centre to find hands-on displays and learn about wetlands. Family events and activities are organised throughout the year. Excellent facilities and programmes make this a popular venue for school visits. Open daily, 9.30am-5pm (4.30pm Nov-Mar). Schools Birthdays **Open all year** Price B **Check out page 50.**

Tetbury(near), **Westonbirt, The National Arboretum,** www.forestry.gov.uk/westonbirt 01666 880220. Explore 600 acres of trees, ranging from giant redwoods to delicate acacias. There are discovery days and trails for children. Open daily, 10am-8pm or dusk if earlier, & in Dec for 'The Enchanted Wood', Fri-Sun, 5-7pm. Schools **Open all year** Price B.

WILTSHIRE

Chippenham(near), **Lackham Country Park,** Wiltshire College Lackham, Lacock, www.lackham.co.uk 01249 466800. Gardens with an animal park, children's laurel maze, museum and woodland trails provide plenty of interest. Special events. Open Easter-Aug, Sun & Bank Hol Mons, 10am-5pm; also Aug, Tues-Thurs. Schools **Price A.**

Cholderton, **Cholderton Rare Breeds Farm Park,** www.rabbitworld.co.uk 01980 629438, offers a variety of attractions. Feed the animals, visit Rabbit World, explore the replica Iron Age farm and try the play areas. Open Spring-Autumn, daily, 10am-6pm, Winter, Sat-Sun, 11am-4pm; please confirm before visiting. Schools Birthdays **Open all year** Price B.

Highworth(near), **Roves Farm,** Sevenhampton, www.rovesfarm.co.uk 01793 763939. Animals to meet and feed, spring lambing, nature trails, indoor and outdoor adventure play and a willow maze. Open Feb half term-Oct half term, days vary (but daily in school hols); also for Christmas. Schools Birthdays **Price B.**

Mere(near), Bush Farm Bison Centre, West Knoyle, www.bisonfarm.co.uk 01747 830263. Herds of bison and elk make this a farm and woodland walk with a difference. In the farmyard are chipmunks, racoons and prairie dogs. Open Apr-Sept, Wed-Sun & Bank Hol Mons, 10am-5pm. Schools Price B.

Swindon(near), Butterfly World, Studley Grange, Wroughton, www.studleygrange.co.uk 01793 852400, is part of the Craft Village. Wander through the tropical house as magical butterflies fly around you. There are fish to feed, a minibeasts house and a cafe. Open daily, 10am-6pm (dusk in Winter). Schools Birthdays **Open all year Price B Check out 'Pottery Painting & Craft Activities' and page 20.**

Teffont, Farmer Giles Farmstead, www.farmergiles.co.uk 01722 716338. Bottle-feed lambs and goats, ride a pony or take a tractor tour at this working farm. Leave time for the huge indoor and outdoor play areas. Open Mar-beg Nov, daily, 10am-5pm; Winter, Sat-Sun, & daily in school hols. Schools Birthdays **Open all year Price B.**

Tollard Royal, Larmer Tree Gardens, Rushmore Estate, www.larmertreegardens.co.uk 01725 516971, have ornamental birds, an adventure playground and an exhibition of colonial buildings with a children's trail. Open Apr-Jun & Aug-Oct, Sun-Thurs, 11am-4pm. **Price B.**

Warminster, Longleat Safari Park, off A36, on A362 Warminster to Frome road, www.longleat.co.uk 01985 844400. Longleat is a great day out for all the family. Discover lions, tigers and giraffe within this world-famous safari park before going on to explore the many attractions combined within the Longleat Passport: Longleat House, the Longleat Hedge Maze, Safari Boats, the Adventure Castle and the Blue Peter Maze, Longleat Railway, Pets Corner, Postman Pat Village and more. A Passport includes one visit to all 11 attractions with the option of returning before the end of the season (6th Nov 2005). Attractions open daily, 12th Feb-6th Nov. Schools **Price G Check out 'History' chapter and page 50.**

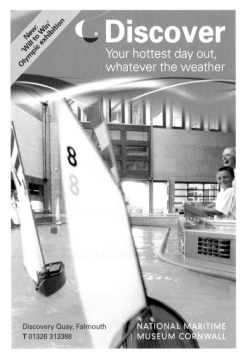

Places to go outside the area

CORNWALL

Falmouth, National Maritime Museum Cornwall, Discovery Quay, www.nmmc.co.uk 01326 313388, offers a maritime experience as exhilarating as the sea and always has new opportunities to encounter famous boats from Olympic gold winners to pioneering explorers. New for 2005 is an exhibition celebrating Team Philips; Pete Goss and team in an amazing world class race aboard a revolutionary 40m long catamaran. Opening in July is one of the UK's largest surfing exhibitions to celebrate the sport and its 'lifestyle'. With a unique natural underwater viewing location, breathtaking views from the 29m tower, hands-on interactives, audio visual immersive experiences, talks and the chance to get out on the water and discover the coastal marine life, this Museum has something for everyone. Use the Park and Float service and sail to the museum in a classic ferry. Open daily, 10am-5pm. Schools **Open all year Price B Check out page 52.**

OXFORDSHIRE

Burford, Cotswold Wildlife Park, www.cotswoldwildlifepark.co.uk 01993 823006, occupies 120 acres of gardens and parkland with a wide variety of animals to be seen. The wildlife varies from reptiles to tarantulas, penguins to rhinos as well as endangered Asiatic lions, Amur leopards and Red Pandas in large enclosures. Children will love to watch the antics of the lively gibbons and meerkats. Extensive shaded picnic lawns also provide the setting for a large adventure playground. A brass-rubbing centre and cafeteria are located in a listed Victorian Manor. Special events are held throughout the summer and a narrow-gauge railway runs from Apr-Oct. Open daily at 10am. Closes 6pm (last admission 4.30pm) Mar-Sept, telephone for winter closing. Schools **Open all year Price C Check out page 52.**

DesignAway, Upton Downs Farm Workshops www.designaway.co.uk 01993 824445, is where children and adults can have great fun decorating a mug or plate, painting a T-shirt or Christmas stocking, and there's lots more to choose from. Exciting new creative courses during school holidays and birthday parties or schools visits can be arranged. Refreshments are also available. Please telephone for opening times, more details or a brochure. Schools Birthdays **Open all year Check out page 55.**

Wigginton Heath, The Water Fowl Sanctuary and Children's Animal Centre, off the A361 Banbury to Chipping Norton Road, 01608 730252. Children will love this friendly, family-run, countryside haven. Throughout the year there are pets and baby animals that can be handled when closely supervised by accompanying adults, and many of the birds can also be fed. See the goats, sheep, ponies, highland cattle, pigs and a donkey, as well as rare breeds of hens, emus, rheas, an ostrich and lots of ducks! There is a children's play area, and plenty of room to picnic in a rural and informal setting. Practical clothing and wellies are a good idea in wet weather. Groups are welcome by prior arrangement with discounts for 10 or more. Open Tues-Sun, School Hol and Bank Hol Mons, 10.30am-5.30pm, or dusk if earlier. **Open all year Price B Check out page 55.**

BERKSHIRE

Windsor, LEGOLAND® www.LEGOLAND.co.uk 08705 040404, set in 150 acres of lovely parkland, offers an exciting and imaginative day out with lots of hands-on, interactive discovery. Look out for three brand new rides opening for 2005. Ride the Jungle Coaster which promises thrills of acceleration, speed and high drops along a wild roller-coaster track that is themed to simulate an automobile test! Exciting experiences await as you wander through the Creation Centre. Discover the Imagination Centre, enter the Traffic area and have a go on the Driving School. Take the younger children to the Waterworks area, watch the daring stunt shows, scale the challenging Climbing Wall, brave the Pirate Falls and explore Miniland, made from over 35 million LEGO® bricks. Open 12th Mar-31st Oct 2005, daily (except some Tues & Wed in Spring & Autumn) from 10am, closing times vary. Schools **Price G Check out page 54.**

LEGOLAND
WINDSOR

5 NEW ATTRACTIONS INCLUDING **3 NEW RIDES**

£5 off
Entry to LEGOLAND® Windsor

2005 Opening Dates
12th March to 30th October

200315

LEGO, the LEGO logo and LEGOLAND are trademarks of the LEGO Group. ©2004 The LEGO Group. SL094 11/04

£5.00 off entry – Excluding August

Terms & Conditions:
- Voucher entitles a maximum of five people to £5.00 off full admission price per person at LEGOLAND Windsor.
- Entrance for children under three years of age is free.
- Voucher must be presented upon entrance into LEGOLAND Windsor.
- Not to be used in conjunction with any other offer, reward/loyalty program, 2 Day Pass, Annual Pass, group booking, on-line tickets, rail inclusive offers or an exclusive event or concert – please call for more information on dates and times.
- Guests are advised that not all attractions and shows may be operational on the day of their visit.
- Height, age and weight restrictions may apply on some rides.
- Guests under the age of 14 or those that do not meet the height restrictions, must be accompanied a person aged 18 or over.
- This is not for re-sale, is non-refundable and non-transferable.
- The park opens for the 2005 season on 12th March and closes on 30th October.
- Voucher is valid for admissions from 12th March to 30th October, excluding the month of August and selected dates – please call in advance to confirm excluded dates.
- This offer is limited to one per household.
- This offer will apply irrespective of the entrance price at the time of use.
- LEGOLAND Windsor will be closed on selected weekdays in March, April, May, September and October.
- PLEASE call www.LEGOLAND.co.uk in advance to confirm dates and prices.

LEGOLA WINDS

FIRE ACA

one of three **NEW RIDES** for 2005

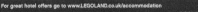

For great hotel offers go to www.LEGOLAND.co.uk/accommodation

LEGOLAND Windsor, Windsor, Berkshire SL4 4AY WWW.LEGOLAND.co.uk

SOMERSET

Cricket St Thomas, The Wildlife Park, www.wild.org.uk 01460 30111. Go wild at Cricket St Thomas, one of Britain's leading centres for wildlife conservation and education. See animals at close quarters, catch a ride on the safari train and spot exotic animals, many of them endangered species. Get close to more familiar furry friends in the Children's Farm! Join a tour with a Keeper and learn about the world of lemurs, as you wander through one of the largest Lemur Woods in the world! Play areas and many activities for children. Visit the website to check for special offers. Open daily, 10am-6pm or 4.30pm in Winter. Schools Birthdays **Open all year Price C Check out page 56.**

SUSSEX

Cambridge Language & Activity Courses. CLAC, www.clac.org.uk 01223 240340, organises interesting Summer courses for 8-13 year and 14-17 year olds at two separate sites in lovely countryside locations, Lavant House and Slindon College, West Sussex. The idea is to bring together British and foreign students to create natural language exchange in a motivated and fun environment. There are French, German and Spanish classes for British students and English for overseas students. Fully supervised in a safe environment, there are lots of activities such as swimming, tennis, team games and competitions, drama and music, in addition to the language tuition. Residential or not, these courses offer enjoyable multi-activity weeks with 20 hours of specific tuition in small groups. Courses run weekly during July and August. Please call for more details and a brochure. Birthdays **Check out page 56.**

Pottery & Fabric Painting

We can fire your imagination and help you to paint something special with pottery or fabrics in our studio near Burford with plenty of free parking.

All ages and school groups welcome. Birthday parties arranged on request from £6 per head. Lots of ideas for fundraising. Commissions undertaken, Holiday Workshops.

Please telephone for opening hours and more details or brochure
Tel: 01993 824445

Upton Downs Farm Workshops
Burford, OXFORDSHIRE OX18 4LY
www.designaway.co.uk

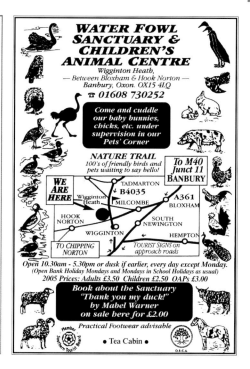

WATER FOWL SANCTUARY & CHILDREN'S ANIMAL CENTRE
Wigginton Heath,
— Between Bloxham & Hook Norton —
Banbury, Oxon. OX15 4LQ
☎ **01608 730252**

Come and cuddle our baby bunnies, chicks, etc. under supervision in our Pets' Corner

NATURE TRAIL
100's of friendly birds and pets waiting to say hello!

To M40 Junct 11 BANBURY

WE ARE HERE Wigginton Heath
B4035 TADMARTON MILCOMBE A361 BLOXHAM
HOOK NORTON SOUTH NEWINGTON
WIGGINTON HEMPTON
TO CHIPPING NORTON TOURIST SIGNS on approach roads

Open 10.30am - 5.30pm or dusk if earlier, every day except Monday.
(Open Bank Holiday Mondays and Mondays in School Holidays as usual)
2005 Prices: Adults £3.50 Children £2.50 OAPs £3.00

Book about the Sanctuary "Thank you my duck!" by Mabel Warner on sale here for £2.00

Practical Footwear advisable
• Tea Cabin •

effects including tropical rain showers, thunder and lightning storms, cascading waterfalls, rainforest mists and a cacophany of wildlife noises! Look out for tropical fish, chattering gorillas, trumpeting elephants, slithering boa and life-sized crocodiles! Reservations can be made at all times with the exception of weekends and school holidays. Open Mon-Fri from 12noon and weekends and holidays from 11.30am. Schools Birthdays **Open all year** Price G **Check out page 57.**

LET'S GO THE THE THEATRE

The Lion King, Lyceum Theatre, Wellington Street, www.thelionking.co.uk 0870 243 9000 (ticket hotline, booking fees apply), 020 7845 0949 (group bookings).
Ingeniously adapted from Disney's classic animated feature film, The Lion King is a spectacular visual feast, which transports audiences to a dazzling world that explodes with glorious colours, stunning effects and enchanting music. At the heart of the show is the powerful and moving story of 'Simba' and the epic adventure of his journey from a wide-eyed cub to his destined role as 'King of the Pridelands'. Audiences all over the world have marvelled at the inspiration that brings the entire African savannah to life on stage, including giraffes, birds, gazelles, antelopes, elephants, cheetahs and zebras. The Lion King's musical score ranges from pulsating African rhythms to contemporary rock, including Tim Rice and Elton John's 'Can You Feel the Love Tonight' and 'Circle of Life'. A show not to be missed. Performances Tues-Sat 7.30pm, Matinees Wed & Sat 2pm, Sun 3pm, Christmas performance times may vary. Schools **Open all year** Price G **Check out page 62.**

Mamma Mia! Prince of Wales Theatre, West End 0870 8500393. This story of a daughter's quest to discover the identity of her father unfolds through ABBA's timeless songs. An enchanting tale of love, laughter and friendship, it is a musical not to be missed. **Open all year** Price G.

The Miz Kids' Club, is an unmissable drama experience where children can go behind the scenes of the brilliant musical, Les Misérables and then enjoy a matinee performance of the show. This is a great opportunity for children to enter the world of theatre and discover the fascination of a big West End production. Back stage, children can hear the story of Les Misérables and learn one of the famous songs, try on the costumes and see the props, join in the drama workshop and improvisation games and even meet a member of the cast. Older children look at the technical operation of the stage effects and focus on characterisation in their improvisation workshop. The clubs meet before the Saturday matinee at 10.30am for 8–11s and 10.45am for 12–15s, both finishing at 1.15pm. Packages, from £28 include a snack packed lunch and a ticket to the performance on the day. For details visit www.lesmis.com or call 0870 8509171. **Open all year Check out page 60.**

The Phantom of the Opera, Her Majesty's Theatre, Haymarket 0207 4945400. This spine tingling tale tells the tragic love story of a beautiful opera singer and a young composer, shamed by his physical appearance into a shadowy existence beneath Paris Opera House. **Open all year** Price G.

LET'S PLAY

Snakes and Ladders, Syon Park, Brentford, www.snakes-and-ladders.co.uk 020 8847 0946, is well signposted from Syon Park or can be accessed via the 237 or 267 bus from Kew Bridge BR or Gunnersbury Underground Station. Children will find action packed fun whatever the weather. They can let off steam in the giant supervised indoor main play frame, intermediate 2-5s area or toddlers area and use the outdoor adventure playground when the sun shines. A mini motor-bike circuit provides an exciting additional activity, while parents can relax in the cafe overlooking the play frame. Open daily, 10am-6pm. All children must wear socks. Schools Birthdays **Open all year** Price A.

'IT LIGHTS UP THE WEST END WITH A BLAZE OF
FABULOUS IMAGINATION'

Evening Standard

DISNEP
PRESENTS

THE LION KING
THE AWARD-WINNING MUSICAL

CALL TODAY 0870 243 9000*

For more information and on-line bookings visit:

www.thelionking.co.uk*

LYCEUM THEATRE

Wellington Street, Covent Garden, London WC2

A Clear Channel Entertainment Venue   *Booking fees apply

©Disney